D1560230

EMBODY YOUR ESSENCE

BREAK PATTERNS OF SUFFERING AND RECLAIM YOUR JOY

JENNIFER GULBRAND

GODDESS GLOW PUBLISHING

Copyright © 2023 by Jennifer Gulbrand

Published by Goddess Glow Publishing

Designed & Created in the USA

First Printing, 2023

ISBN -979-8-98775-590-7
eBook ISBN - 979-8-98775-591-4

Library of Congress Cataloguing in Publication Date

Names: Jennifer Gulbrand, Author

Title: Embody Your Essence

Description: 1st Edition, Boston, MA

Subject: Self-Actualization, Spiritual, Growth and Healing

Manufactured in the United States of America

Book Design by Robin Garstka

Cover Photo by Ali Rosa

DEDICATION

This book is dedicated to you, for choosing courage over comfort, for releasing what no longer serves you, and for owning your story, so you can more fully embody your soul's essence and radiate your light out into the world.

The Mystery of She

Her heart was connected to the flowers,
as they opened, so did She.
Her voice was connected to the birds,
as they sang, so did She.
Her wisdom was connected to the trees,
as they whispered, so did She.
Her womb was connected to the moon,
as it waxed and waned, so did She.
Her attachments were connected to the tides.
as they let go, so did She.
Her passions were connected to the fire,
as it was stoked, so was She.
Her eyes were connected to the sky,
as it saw things clearly, so did She.
Her emotions were connected to the rivers,
as it flowed, so did She.
Her spirit was connected to the stars,
as they shone, so did She.
Her soul was connected to the entire Universe,
as it expanded, so did She.

Rebecca Campbell

TABLE OF CONTENTS

FORWARD

My inspiration for writing this book came from deep contemplation regarding my own life and a desire to develop more conscious connections with the people in my life. After nearly six decades in this energy body, I realized that when we show up authentically, expose our vulnerabilities, and share our real stories, we begin to heal ourselves and one another.

Henry David Thoreau said, "We are constantly being invited to be who we are," but how many of us accept the invitation to show up authentically in our interactions with others? How often do we feel safe enough to bring our whole self to a conversation or to a relationship? Why don't we go deeper in our interactions with one another?

In a world where people are hiding to stay "safe," speaking our vulnerable truth is one of the most courageous things we can do. I want to serve as a catalyst for a movement toward being more consciously connected—to a place where we find the courage to show up with empathy, authenticity, a recognition of shared values and common experiences, and a safe, supportive container in which to share who we really are at our deepest layers.

Conscious connections are made when we share the unfiltered essence of ourselves with others, including our true identities—not just our joys, but our pain, thoughts, feelings, life experiences, dreams, and desires.

Studies confirm that our brains are hardwired to reach out and interact with other people. Receptors light up when we interact intimately and honestly with friends, family, and community. When we make meaningful connections with other people, we strengthen our immune system, recover from disease faster, and live longer. Meaningful human connection lowers our rates of anxiety, depression, and suicide.

So why do we keep our truths locked in a vault for most of our life, feeling lost, alone, and broken, disconnected from ourselves and one another? I believe we are held back by our own subconscious limiting beliefs and fears of being misunderstood, of being judged, and not belonging.

Here I am, showing up in my wholeness, to reveal my true essence—who I am, what I have experienced, and how those experiences have shaped my life—with the intention of helping others on their path to healing.

The shift that will lead us to deeper, more fulfilling relationships and connectedness will happen when we begin looking at our commonalities and recognizing our shared experiences. What a difference we will make when we show up authentically with a desire to listen and learn and be fully present for one another through more conscious and connected communications, receptivity, and understanding.

Held by the Earth.
Moved by the Moon.
Sparked by the Sun.
Swayed by the Sea.
She was a force to be reckoned with.

-Rebecca Campbell

WELCOME TO MY SACRED CIRCLE

BEAUTIFUL SOUL

It's no accident that you have found your way here. I'm quite certain you have been divinely guided to this book for a reason. This is the very moment when you realize that there is only one remarkable YOU in the Universe and you deserve to revel in your own radiance and truth.

I wholeheartedly believe that it's never too late to move beyond life's challenges and rise out of the ashes to embody your soul's essence more fully. By "essence," I am referring to your dharma, your intrinsic human design, your divine reason for being here. What does it mean to embody your essence? We embody our essence when we fully inhabit, embrace, and express our true nature.

It means you can unravel your entire life story, to discover who you are at a soul level, and to fulfill your purpose in this energy body. When we embody our true nature, we can learn to break the patterns of suffering and reclaim our joy!

No matter what you have been through to get here, take a deep, expansive breath, then slowly and mindfully release and let go. Inhale, rinse, repeat. Open your heart space and receive all the love and learning coming your way.

I am willing to bet that you are in a time of radical re-awakening. You are showing up ready to listen and respond to the cravings of the heart, to release what doesn't serve you, to feel and move through what needs healing, and to own your story.

I hold the heart-centered intention to be a Teacher and a Warrior of Love, Embodiment, and Empowerment for you and for all women everywhere. After thirty-five years of leading businesses in the health and wellness space, I have found my calling as a builder of communities and safe, supportive containers designed to promote growth and healing. I am here now, showing up authentically, doing my part to help heal the human heart and raise the collective vibration one woman at a time.

I am honored to meet you where you are at to hold this space for you in my sacred circle. I encourage you to embark on a path of self-discovery and to reconnect with your sacred feminine power and own your truth.

As humans, we are programmed to conform to the expectations of our culture and of the people closest to us, including parents and caregivers. We take on the expectations and judgments of those around us, as well as their perceptions of who we are. As a result, these stories get deeply embedded into our subconscious. Because we are socialized to belong, we do whatever it takes to keep up with the script that has been written for us, even when it does not align with our true nature. When we can transform our wounds, heal, and create space for self-love, we learn that we are here to understand ourselves, not to be understood by others.

For years, I never really felt like I belonged anywhere here on earth. I have come to understand that I am here, in this lifetime, to share my experiences and learnings to guide others to finding the strength to move through their challenges and find their light.

Like many of us, I lived most of my life on autopilot, succumbing to societal patriarchal structures and inequalities as well as my own inner critic. I have been through the mud and sat in the thick of it, feeling "stuck" more times than I can remember. I suffered early childhood trauma piled on top of ancestral and gestational trauma already contained within my energy body. I buried my wounds of abandonment and self-loathing so deeply that nobody could see my scars. I even hid them from myself.

I accepted situations in my life that were not in my highest and best good. I stayed in unhealthy relationships out of fear.

I operated from a subconscious belief system that I was responsible for every bad thing that had happened to me and hid under blankets of guilt and shame. These emotional burdens negatively impacted my well-being and sabotaged many of my relationships.

In time, as a survival mechanism, I learned to shape-shift and behave in overly extroverted ways that were outside of my true nature, fighting to be seen and heard to prove my worth. My thoughts, emotions, and actions were being led by more masculine "doing" tendencies to push forward, resist, and get sh*t done, rather than honoring my sacred feminine energy of "being," receiving, and allowing things to flow. I was out of balance and alignment, and it kept me stuck for a better part of my life.

Does this sound familiar?

- Do you present yourself as confident and having it all together while feeling lost and not good enough on the inside?

- Are you being held back by self-doubt and fear?

- Are you ready to release what no longer serves you?

- Do you want to make choices that are more aligned with your true nature?

Like most women, we are taught to put on our big girl pants and smile and tell the world, and ourselves, that everything is "fine." But it's not always fine, and it's okay not to be fine. This is the conversation we need to start having with one another. Bring on the truth tellers so we can all feel less alone and lock arms to learn, grow, and evolve together.

It was not until my fifties that I gradually began to awaken and focus on the fact that I was solely responsible for my own life and experiences. I realized that I am not defined by my wounds. I made a conscious decision to save myself by moving through the pain and suffering to find my essence, my truth.

I mindfully untangled from limiting beliefs and subconscious stories that had blocked my progress for so many years. I stopped looking outside of myself for acceptance and acknowledgement and began recognizing my own value. I stopped living in the past and committed to doing what was necessary to heal from my traumatic experiences, to become more fully embodied and empowered, and to redirect my life. I vowed to choose courage over fear, and everything changed for me. My relationships with others improved greatly, because I was able to gently release expectations and focus on my own well-being.

I began to find my true self again. I re-engaged with intuitive gifts I had forgotten I had—by that, I mean a deep connection to Spirit that had been shut down in my early childhood because, at that time, nobody around me could understand or validate what that even meant. Learning to quiet my mind long enough to listen enabled me to tap into my own inner knowing and find my way back to myself after years of believing that I was unworthy of love.

I learned to practice compassionate detachment and the importance of separating myself from socially defined roles and responsibilities that put everyone else's needs before my own. I began to look inward for the purest of love that I held for myself, rather than relying on the old patterns of expecting it from everyone around me. I got back into the flow and became more aligned with my dharma.

Every one of us has been through loss, tragedy, and pain and is carrying subconscious limiting beliefs that hold us back from being fully realized. As humans, most of us hide behind our pain and shame because we fear how we will be received or perceived. There is life-changing energy that comes with the act of lightening up. The release. When you own your story, identify limiting beliefs, and replace them with new mindsets, you start to feel the shift. You start loving yourself again and believing that you are valuable and worthy of all good things coming your way.

My intention is to support you and other women with your own conscious re-awakening and to encourage you to trust your inner wisdom and connect more deeply to yourself so you can live a more meaningful and flourishing life here on earth.

I'm still learning, evolving, and practicing what I teach others. I am here now, ready to show up in my bigness without fear about how I may be perceived. This is my truth. There is only one me, with my own unique story that has everything to do with who I am.

Allow me to take you on a journey back to yourself as we explore being in our humanness and the many beautiful ways of living forward with more joy, ease, and alignment.

We all have the power to choose and to create positive change in our lives. My wish for you is that you will find the courage to stop hiding, start healing, and radiate your own light out into the world. I am living proof that it is never too late to lighten up and begin again.

You can choose courage or
you can choose comfort.
You cannot have both.

-Brené Brown

THE ENERGY SHIFT

I believe BIG universal energy shifts are occurring and that women are being called to step up, stop playing small, and consciously show up for themselves and one another in a heart-centered way. There is something deeply spiritual that is stirring up a new wave of intense energies as part of a global awakening of the planet.

This change we sense is a rise in sacred feminine energy, I'm guessing you can feel the momentum building. It's a new dawn, a time for women to walk into the light more authentically and more boldly than ever before...to be seen and heard for who they truly are on a deeper soul level. The time is now for women to come together and help raise the collective vibration of the world.

Can you feel it?

Women everywhere are experiencing the shift. Doors are opening and new opportunities are presenting themselves to us both personally and professionally. We can really be whoever we want to be and do the kind of work that we truly desire to do to make a difference in our own lives and in the lives of others.

Times are changing, and we are here to lead humanity forward to a new way of being. It's time to awaken a new era of sisterhood on the planet.

This is an invitation to manifest something extraordinary. This new energy is asking you to connect with the most sacred part of yourself—your inner goddess. Her feminine energy is soft, nurturing, and intuitive, but also strong, wise, and powerful. She is the best part of you. She is inside of you and connects you to Source. To the Divine or the Universe or your higher soul self, however you define a greater power. Embrace her in a warm hug.

As an Intuitive, Reiki Master Teacher and Sound Healing Facilitator, I am all about vibration and frequency. As we experience this wider shift in universal life force energy, it's important to tune into the rhythms of your own biofield—your body's electrical system in its entirety—both the electric current that runs through your body, and the magnetic field that surrounds it. The vibrations within you and around you are connected with your conscious and subconscious mind, including your memories. Learning to sense your own vibrations as well as the energy of others is something worth exploring.

Let's approach this feminine energy as a universal quality in consciousness. This is a calling for us to stand united together, individually, and collectively, and embrace this new stage in human evolution. We have everything we need to create, inspire, connect, and evolve as a human race, and it's up to us to lead the way. I am deeply grateful to the soul sisters traveling on this consciousness path with me who are helping to pave the path forward for the next generations of women to follow.

She's learning to recognize
more and more what's
best for her vibration.
She's honoring it and
using it to guide her higher daily.
Her soul is at peace and
vibrating higher,
because of her dedication
and reclaimed ownership
of her vibration.

-Lalah Delia

WHAT'S RISING UP IN YOU?

Chances are you were drawn to this book because you feel a gravity pulling you forward. . .a desire to manifest something big and bold in your life.

Perhaps there is something coming alive inside of you, but you are feeling unsure what it is and, even more importantly, what to do with it. Perhaps you are feeling unsettled? Undervalued? Misunderstood? Do you feel as though the old you may be disappearing one day at a time? Are you confused about where you're going as though you've lost your way? Do you feel "stuck"? Do you spend time ruminating on a deep seeded desire to:

- transition out of a job that no longer inspires you?
- reinvent yourself in a new light?
- surround yourself with more like-minded people?
- attract relationships where you feel more seen?
- escape current reality to begin your life all over again somewhere new?
- seek more depth and meaning in everyday life?

Or maybe all the above?

I recognize these stirrings well! They relate to my own story and to the stories of so many other women who share similar shifts as part of the current energy surrounding us.

So many of us get to a place in our lives where we feel called to change but are stopped in our tracks by fear—fear of making a mistake, of being alone, of being judged, of rejection by family and friends. It's time to let go of the chains that bind us and break free. Now is the time for your radical awakening.

These experiences that so many women are having are what prompted me to do the work I do and to ultimately share my story. I support women just like you who are feeling paralyzed and unsure where to begin. I'm humbled and honored to be working with women in life's transition who are experiencing a conscious awakening.

We need to start sharing our raw, personal experiences with one another so we can rise and support a new direction for other women, young and old alike, so they too can join the rising.

When we tap into our sacred feminine and the energetic qualities that define us as women, we have access to a whole new source of power that is unstoppable. I'm living proof that it is never too late to change the course of your life.

Rise up, Soul Sister, and show the world your radiance! You are a divine and sacred being, and you alone hold the power to uplevel your own life. It begins with that first deep breath and a commitment to yourself to do whatever it takes to follow your heart.

Women are abandoning
the need to just come
together and gossip.
They are coming together
to heal, grow, and prosper.
This is the new sisterhood.

-Marquita Williams

YOU ARE NOT ALONE

The most important message I want to share is that you are not alone, you are not broken, and you do not need to be fixed.

There are millions of women around the globe experiencing this massive shift of energy and vibration. It is not something to fear but to be fully and wildly embraced.

I've met and worked with many women—writers, artists, coaches, healers, photographers, designers, financial planners, spiritual healers, and serial entrepreneurs—all of whom are feeling restless and ready for change. We're living in a brave new world after having survived a worldwide pandemic and the mental health fallout left behind in its wake. People everywhere are cracking wide open in unfamiliar and expansive ways. It is very invigorating to be experiencing this remarkable energy and this defining time in history when more and more people are awakening in this way.

Endless possibilities are presenting themselves to women in every aspect of life. Fragments from the broken glass ceiling are falling out like confetti and creating an entirely new landscape for women to step more authentically onto the world stage. We celebrate a kick-ass team of women in powerful positions who are changing the conversations and making history.

As women living in a modern world, our individual and collective voices need to be heard. Our ideas need to be respected and put into action. Our messages of kindness and acceptance need to be valued so we can lead the charge in creating a better world.

The struggle to find the right balance between career and family for women is still very real, but even that cannot stop us now. I believe we are being called to live more fulfilling lives by being a part of this movement. We are leading the way for all of humanity to create a beautiful, loving, and more peaceful way of being and you are here to be an important part of it.

We are the sum of all
people we have ever met.
You change the tribe,
and the tribe changes you.

-Dirk Wittenborn

WHY WOMEN NEED A TRIBE

A tribe is generally defined as a community of people linked together by family ties, ethnicity, and/or religion. However, tribes are not limited to people who are related. They can be a group of people who share the same beliefs and ideologies or shared missions. I believe that women need a tribe of other women to feel fully supported, which inspired me to create the SheBreathes Balance Women's Collaborative in 2016, an education, empowerment, and advocacy initiative holding space for women to lift one another up personally and professionally.

Long before the over-scheduled work week and the isolating days of social media, women lived in cultures where they supported one another in all aspects of life. Together they raised and protected children, foraged for food, and helped each other through life's daily challenges. As humans and technology evolved, women became more independent, and the time previously dedicated to togetherness became less important—or so it seemed.

Sadly, we are socialized to compare ourselves with other women and to compete, yet our true nature is one of collectivism.

Studies show that women are designed to connect with each other. In times of stress or need, women release oxytocin, a hormone that compels one to nurture and bond. These bonds result in positive mental, physical, and emotional well-being and restore women to their true nature.

Like so many women, I spent so much of my life feeling isolated, alone, fearful, and not good enough to show up authentically as me. I charged through life hiding my beliefs about my own inadequacy under this tough, "I have it all together" exterior, rarely showing my true self, and being too afraid to share parts of my story.

Why do we all live like this when it would be so much more beneficial to show up, to let go of social constraints, to reveal who we really are by sharing our truths with one another? I'm determined to help promote a world where people can feel safe to unbound themselves from the chains, to heal and move forward.

I often bring a group of women together for a social event at my studio, like a networking event or a dinner. Each of the women will show up dressed to impress and ready to exchange pleasantries and make on-the-surface connections with other like-minded women. These gatherings typically begin with some small talk about their business. But then something special unfolds as they begin to realize that they are in a safe, supportive container where they are encouraged to let their guards down and get real with one another.

Every single time I hold space like this, it's inevitable that one brave soul will begin to share something vulnerable about her personal life, perhaps her parenting struggles, or events from her troubled childhood and it's like a magical unwinding begins to unfold as everyone realizes it's okay to show up authentically, to shed some tears, and to share their own stories. This is where the connectedness and interconnectedness begin.

I receive some of my greatest satisfaction in hearing from women how the SheBreathes Collaborative has changed their lives for the better. Women ranging from age eighteen to eighty have felt seen, heard, and validated by being a part of our community. I have witnessed the remarkable change in so many women who say they feel like themselves again when they show up more authentically and in support of one another. It is my honor to be holding space in this way and I am deeply humbled. I love my tribe.

But in today's disconnected and demanding world, how do you find a tribe of like-hearted people who have your back?

Here are some suggestions on where to start:

Look for people with common interests and values.

Seek out like-minded women who share your interests and will expand your universe. Take a class, join a wellness studio, attend local meet-up groups, and start making meaningful connections.

Identify your wants and needs.

Ask yourself, "What personal need do I want to fulfill?" Be truthful in your answer and leave self-doubt and judgment at the door. Follow your heart and the universe will attract compatible individuals.

Surround yourself with people who lift you up.

Share your time with women who have your best interest at heart. Be part of a group that not only celebrates one another's successes, but also helps each other weather the storms.

Be yourself.

It's easy to confuse what we think we like with what we like. Different people have different interests, values, and goals. Be authentic and stay true to your beliefs, and your vibe will attract your tribe.

Trust your instincts.

Finding your tribe may feel scary, but trust yourself. Your heart and mind will know you've made that special connection and found your soul sisters.

I know from personal and professional experience that, when women come together with a shared intention, amazing things happen. When we create a supportive environment to laugh, explore, and share genuine experiences, we strengthen our community and raise the collective vibration of our world.

Your High Vibe Tribe is waiting for you!

*When we raise our vibrational
frequencies to Light, we uplift
the collective consciousness
into higher dimensions.*

-Unknown

THE COLLECTIVE RISING

I spend a great deal of my time having transformational conversations with women who are facing life's transitions. Whether they are recent graduates trying to discover their passion, new moms trying not to lose themselves in the chaos, highly ambitious business professionals, or empty nesters redis-covering what lights them up in their third act of life, these are the women who are learning to walk in their own unique beauty, with strength and courage. These are the women look-ing to reclaim their divine feminine power and level up.

Women everywhere are awakening to a new level of consciousness and rising up to have their voices heard, many for the first time.

The thing that happens when women awaken is that they learn to honor themselves in new ways. This self-honor-ing allows us people to create different standards for their lives. And, while this awakening is not always easy, it is a vital part of our individual and collective evolution.

This book is not about women rising up over men. It is about remembering that every woman is sacred and deserv-ing. It's in recognition of the fact that the sacred and divine feminine is returning and rising just as she should. We have been suppressed for far too long.

Women have suffered 5,000+ years of male dominance, and that has resulted in our trying to behave more like the typical Western man —leading with our doing energy—as we drive, compete, and push through life to get things done while disregarding and closing off our more feminine qualities.

Now is the time to bring about a balance between the feminine and masculine energies within us, and in our world, as part of the global healing movement. We need both ways of "doing" and "being" to get back into energetic harmony and balance.

Many of us get to a point in our lives when we feel a yearning for something more—cravings of the heart—to live life more authentically and in better alignment with our soul's calling. And when we get real with ourselves, we become change makers, disruptors, and revolutionary leaders who challenge and overturn old ways of being. We naturally begin to seek out other people who are traveling on a similar consciousness path to help us forge new roads forward.

We are not meant to do this alone and divided. Even though our patriarchal society has socialized us, as women, to compete and compare, we know that when women come together, amazing things begin to unfold. We heal and thrive in communities because we are designed to be connected. WE. NEED. ONE. OTHER.

It is time to expand from an individual to a collective consciousness. By invoking more of the Sacred Feminine tendencies in all of us, we can imagine a world where people display qualities of love, connection, and harmony to build a better word, to move into a new phase of evolution together.

Women have been gathering in circles for centuries seeking meaningful connection and healing, because we inherently know that when we gather in safe, supportive spaces, we can create positive and powerful change.

Together, we are boundless, with no end to our capabilities. When we make the conscious decision to rise, our support team naturally assembles, and we are connected to a constellation of soul sisters, to an ocean of women rising right alongside us. Then, when we feel safe and supported, there's an unwinding that happens. A release. A softening. An opening. An expansion.

I believe that when we co-create with conscious, like-hearted people, in safe, supportive communities, we can design experiences that benefit both the individual and the collective.

Together we can imagine a world that is healed with respect and understanding and with a strong sense of community that fosters kindness, acceptance, and grace.

We all have access to the fullest expression of human potential to create a world that we desire. The possibilities that lie ahead are endless. This is where the magic happens. This is where the deep healing and evolution begins.

The dance between
darkness and light
will always remain.
The stars and the moon
will always need the
darkness to be seen.
The darkness will not be
worth having without the
moon and the stars.

-C. JoyBell C.

BEING IN
OUR HUMANNESS

OPPOSING FORCES

Before we can heal and emerge as a fully embodied and empowered woman, we need to examine some of the external elements that impact us on our journey called life.

Our human condition is puzzling in that it's a bit like being bumped about on a crazy, twisty carnival ride. Up one moment and down the next. One day, we're flying high because everything is amazing, and then it's not and we feel as though there is no way to navigate our way out of the thick of it. We ride the tumultuous waves of give and take away, white and black, light and dark, day and night, yin and yang, male and female, right and left, and what we often associate all of this as good vs. evil in our search for an ailment for the motion sickness that comes from this tumultuousness.

Where we are at any given moment can shift in an instant and significantly impact our sense of well-being. Our human existence is driven by what we perceive as opposing forces—the light and the shadow—and we feel the pull of how the two furiously compete for airtime.

There are those remarkable moments of pure, unencumbered joy when everything sparkles. Moments when our soul-searching spirits keep moving us toward more light because of the way it makes us feel-alive, vital, abundant, and powerful-the reminders that life is indeed beautiful, fulfilling and well worth living.

Then there are the moments that shake us to our very core, knock us to our knees, and plummet our soul into deepest, darkest shadows. Evil, selfishness, envy, greed, anger, and fear can lurk inside of all of us. Moments that can feel like we're drowning in the muck and leave us gasping for air.

We often become aware of our shadows when they lead us into conflicts with other people. On other occasions, they show themselves as feelings of guilt or depression. We are even capable of projecting these shadows onto others because we can't accept that these emotions and thoughts belong to us and are shaped by our own limiting beliefs.

We are programmed from early childhood to hide behind our grief and shame...to bury what we see as failures, rather than facing the demons head on with the intention to release and heal. We see it as simply a part of being human to keep these shadows locked deeply inside of us. But that, my friends, is not the way to healing. We need to feel it and move through it to heal it. We'll be exploring that in a later chapter.

It's important to face our shadows, to name them, and to get to know them intimately. We are human and accepting ourselves in our totality will help us develop a healthy self-esteem and live a better and more balanced life. We need to learn to recognize that the light and shadows go hand in hand.

Light cannot exist without dark; in fact, they are complementary rather than oppositional. Both are necessary phases of the life cycle that together are perceived as harmonious totality.

Perhaps this civilized experience we are all having is less about avoiding the dark and craving the light. Perhaps it's more about accepting all of it as being part of being human and the way to being a whole and complete person.

What if we could create many more balanced moments, ones where consciously and mindfully drop from our heads to our hearts and feel and experience everything? Staying grounded in our physical bodies, feet firmly planted on Mother Earth, so we can be more present and mindful of what is—here and now light and dark, happy and sad—what if we could learn to accept it, take it all in, move through it, and still find little things to be grateful for?

While we all crave more light, most of us spend a better part of our time sitting in the shadows and darkness, feeling weighed down by expectations, responsibilities, and limiting beliefs about who we should be, how we should and should not behave, and how we want others to perceive us.

This burden is heavy, and the weight of all these expectations—the "shoulds" and "should nots"—can be soul-crushing. Instead of individual beings who have come here to experience this life as fully as possible, we can get very caught up in the downward spiral of expectations. Sadly, this phenomenon will hold you back from being in your light, from being a fully connected and embodied, wild, and free expression of YOU, at a soul level.

My guess is you have felt the inner conflict yourself... the sheer exhaustion from trying to follow the script handed to you in childhood. All this time you've been efforting to prove your self-worth and value to the world, suppressing the urge to reveal the real you who lies just beneath the surface, the true essence of you that only you know, someone bursting at the seams to be seen and heard.

It is no surprise that we spend so much time hiding in the shadows. As women, we are socialized from a young age to make ourselves smaller to "fit into a mold" that society deems appropriate. Don't be too loud, too proud, too smart, too attractive, or too successful, because when you arrive at these destinations, there will be others there waiting who want to tear you down so quickly your head will spin.

For this reason, it can be difficult to stay in the shiny moments because, all too often, our own unique individuality gets squashed before we can exercise our god(dess)-given opportunity to step into our own true light.

*Be yourself, not your idea of what
you think somebody else's idea
of yourself should be.*

-Henry David Thoreau

WHY CAN'T WE BE REAL?

Can you relate to this feeling of being held back from your true wants and desires?

Have you ever felt like you were playing a role in a movie and having trouble relating with your character?

Or like you are a wind-up doll performing on demand with absolutely no control over your actions?

Most of us arrive at a turning point in our lives when we realize that we are living WAY out of alignment with our true nature and that doing so is causing us to experience imbalance and dis-ease in our physical, energetic, and emotional body. Sometimes we ignore the signs for so long that our body needs to shout at us... LISTEN UP AND PAY ATTENTION!

- Why are we so disconnected from our inner knowing?
- Why don't we pay closer attention to our own needs?
- Why do we hide behind guilt, shame, and feelings of being "not good enough" for the better part of our lives?
- Why is it so difficult to simply honor what is real and true to us?
- What prevents us from stepping onto the stage boldly and proudly, as our one and only self, in our own beautiful skin, with confidence and joy?

We always hear this concept of letting things go, but what if instead we embrace whatever it is that may be blocking us or keeping us stuck and simply learn to let it in so we can address it once and for all and move on?

We all know that when we resist circumstances or situations, they only fester and take deeper root in our emotional and physical bodies. On the contrary, when we accept whatever is with open arms and hearts, and allow it to pass through us, we can get in touch with our raw and true emotions.

We need to give all of those less than positive experiences the attention they deserve to truly heal and transform our lives. That process of being in it, rather than burying it, may take days, weeks, months or even years to process, but in the end, we can rewrite the story and live forward.

What if we could learn to lighten up by letting it all in?

...to stop running from the shadows

...to face our deepest wounds and give them the attention they deserve

...to free ourselves from the limiting beliefs that keep us "stuck"

...to release the guilt and shame

...to unravel old scripts line by line and get to the heart of our true nature

...to feel, learn, grow, and heal

...to show up for all of it

...to consciously embody life in our true essence and experience more joy!!!!

When we can let it all in, before trying to let it go, we learn to live a lighter and less encumbered existence.

The world would be a more beautiful place if we could all just show up authentically for all of it... to live life being more consciously and fully embodied in our humanness.

Sometimes you're not going to feel okay, because that is part of being human. When those times come, and the feelings start to surface, try to allow yourself to feel whatever it is that is coming up for you because you need to feel it to move through it.

Give yourself grace and permission to:

- cry all the tears you need to cry. Scream at the top of your lungs.
- fall on your knees and surrender. Pray if you pray.
- find stillness in meditation. Breathe deeply and completely.
- wrap your arms around a tree and connect to Mother Earth.
- journal it out onto the pages and then burn it.

Do WHATEVER it takes to release the stuck energy and return to the parts of you that you may have forgotten or suppressed.

Allow yourself to feel it all of it, to walk through the pain, frustration, anger, and the tears until you can return to peace on the other side.

What is stopping you?

Our deepest fear is not that
we are inadequate.
Our deepest fear is that we are
powerful beyond measure.
It is our light, not our darkness,
that most frightens us.
We ask ourselves
"Who am I to be brilliant, gorgeous,
talented, fabulous?
Who are you not to be?

-Marianne Williamson

WHAT'S FEAR GOT TO DO WITH IT?

Let me guess. Is it FEAR that is stopping you? It is the one thing that tends to entangle us all.

So much of what prohibits us from standing in our own truth and living an embodied life in full alignment with our higher calling begins and ends with fear.

Fear is a natural, powerful, and primitive human emotion, a sort of survival mechanism we have created in our minds and bodies.

According to psychology research, fear involves a universal biochemical response and a high individual emotional response. It alerts us to the presence of danger or the threat of harm, whether that danger is physical or psychological.

Sometimes fear stems from real threats, but it can also originate from imagined dangers. While fear is a natural response to some situations, it can also lead to distress and disruption when extreme or out of proportion to the actual threat.

And, of course, fear feels real as hell when we are facing it, doesn't it?

But in all actuality, fear is just an illusion—something we create in our imagination.

F.E.A.R.

○ False. Evidence. Appearing. Real.

○ Forgetting Everything About Reality

○ Face Everything and Recover

○ Face it. Embrace it. Replace it.

○ F*ck Everything and Run

Fear is not tangible. It does not exist. More importantly, it certainly does not hold the power over us that we give it. Yet, most of us spend a better part of our lives paralyzed by it, unable to put one foot in front of the other in the direction of what calls to us.

Fear gets lodged in our physical and emotional bodies. It vibrates our nervous systems and lays low until something triggers it, then feelings of anxiety and tension bubble up to the surface without warning.

Have you felt rumblings beating inside of your chest so loudly that you want to burst, and yet you realize they cannot be heard by anyone around you?

Have you found yourself in a spiral of self-sabotage and wondered how you got there? The real question is, how do you plan to break the cycle and get out of this self-imposed prison?

We all struggle with our own ego and our inability to get out of our own way. It is part of the human experience. We justify fear as being important, as it alerts us to the presence of danger or the threat of harm from real dangers. Or do those dangers exist only in our imagination?

These perceived threats take over and begin to control us. We give those thoughts and emotions so much power that they hold us like chained prisoners in our own mind. Perhaps our fear is driven by the sheer magnitude of the possibilities?

We know, on a soul level, that if we begin the process of disrupting the normal standards, pushed upon us from a young age, the force of our own power is beyond comprehension.

I'm here to encourage you to push past your fears and be okay with failing from time to time. Create a new habit of going outside your comfort zone. Let go of old unlimiting beliefs and create the life you desire like your life depends on it, because it does!

Fear is an important human emotion that can help protect us from danger and prepare you to act, but it can also lead to longer-lasting feelings of anxiety. Finding ways to control your fear can help you better cope with these feelings and prevent anxiety from taking hold. We discuss some ways to manage and overcome it in the pages ahead, but practicing mindfulness, seeking support, and making your overall well-being a priority are the best places to start.

Limitless potential exists
within each of us,
but it often goes unrealized
because of our
subconscious limiting beliefs.

-Jenn Gulbrand

LIMITING BELIEFS

Most of us carry old programming that impedes our growth and maturation. The only way to move through these blocks is to see right through them. This work is not easy, but it's important, so let's dive in.

Limiting beliefs, sometimes known as core beliefs, are unconscious stories and judgments we carry about ourselves that define our sense of self. These stories also determine how we feel about others, how happy we are with ourselves, and how we perceive the world at large.

Our core beliefs are even responsible for how successful we are in self-actualizing our deepest desires and in finding meaning in our lives. All too often, we're plagued by those limiting beliefs, which are mostly subconscious and developed between the ages of 0 and 7.

For example, you may have been taught from a young age that achievement results in approval, and that approval makes you successful and deserving of joy. Therefore, if you don't continuously receive outside confirmation of success, you feel unworthy. On a subconscious level, you adopt a self-limiting belief, like "the wants and needs of others are more important than my own."

Limiting beliefs result in you acting for the sake of serving others, usually to attain or preserve their love, affection, or approval. Chances are those actions probably are not in alignment with your divine feminine self and are not serving your highest good. Take a moment to reflect on some examples of limiting beliefs we might hold for ourselves.

I am _____

Unworthy	Unlovable	Worthless
Fearful	Undeserving	Weak
Undesirable	Not Enough	Unwanted
Alone	Unsuccessful	Invisible

Our beliefs about ourselves, our life, and the people in it shape our every moment. The more we believe, the more we can be imprisoned by those beliefs. The more we adhere to beliefs, the more we become attached to them and, as we will discuss a bit later, attachment to any of our beliefs is the root of all suffering.

Our core beliefs frame who we are and how we show up every day. If we stay stuck in those old limiting belief systems that we have created for ourselves, we will remain powerless. If you feel unlovable, you will not attract love. If you ruminate on your lack of financial wealth, you will not attract abundance.

If you feel unworthy, you will never measure up to expectations you've set for yourself. So how can you make the shift for yourself? It begins with identifying your limiting beliefs and then working to find emotional liberation where you can remove the blocks and be in the present moment in its raw, natural state of wonder.

--oo ⋅)(⋅ oo--

Reflections

Take time to reflect and write down what you believe to be YOUR self-limiting beliefs about yourself. Perhaps you wish to focus on one area of your life where you feel really stuck? Who or what are you blaming for your situation?

_____

_____

_____

_____

_____

_____

_____

_____

Next, on a scale of 1 to 10, write next to the belief how much do you believe it to be true. Challenge your core beliefs and prove them to be flawed and unrealistic.

Have compassion for yourself as you work through these core beliefs one at a time. Place a hand on your heart and name the emotions that are coming up for you. Breathe deeply and feel into this emotion and then replace it with a new story.

For example, if you have the core belief "I am unlovable," you might like to replace it with "I am surrounded by loving relationships that nurture me." Or if your core belief is, "I am not successful," you might replace it with "I am full of potential and on the way to reaching my dreams."

_____

_____

_____

_____

_____

_____

_____

You are connecting with your deeper truth about yourself through this practice. As you work toward shifting this negative energy and replacing it with your deeper truth, remember that loving yourself is the key to moving forward. Now, reflect on how your new core belief transforms your life. How will it help you to be more joyful, confident, creative, or prosperous?

_____

_____

_____

_____

_____

_____

_____

_____

_____

_____

_____

_____

Being able to feel safe
with other people is probably
the single most important aspect
of mental health; safe connections
are fundamental to meaningful
and satisfying lives.

-Bessel Van der Kolk

LET'S TALK TRAUMA

So where do limiting beliefs come from, and how are they even formed?

In many cases, the root cause of our limiting beliefs and sub-conscious stories in our heads stems from trauma or what are often called "painful life events." There are all types of traumas, including ancestral, gestational, birth and traumatic incidents that occur during our lifetime from birth on and into a particular lifetime here on earth.

Trauma is a pervasive problem one experiences after being exposed to an incident or series of events that are emotionally disturbing and/or life-threatening. This suffering can have a lasting adverse effect on a person's mental, physical, social, emotional, and/or spiritual well-being.

When we talk about trauma, many of us immediately think about life-altering events like terrorist attacks, mass shootings, natural disasters, and worldwide pandemics. However, trauma can also include less obvious experiences like losing a loved one, being raised in an unstable environment, verbal, physical or sexual abuse, emotional or physical neglect, alcohol/drug exposure, poverty, seeing someone get hurt, bullying, racism, or discrimination—everyday occurrences that are part of the human experience, yet traumatic nonetheless.

Life is full of painful events that test us, and most people have experienced trauma in one way or another. Yet many of us do not think of our experiences as being traumatic. We brush them off with a "it's just life attitude," failing to realize the impact of the events we have endured. Every one of us has lived through traumatic events, whether we recognize it or not.

But with some quiet reflection, I'm sure you can recall specific incidents that challenged your understanding of the world, shook your confidence, eroded your sense of safety, or left you feeling isolated and alone. Those incidents, my friends, are characterized as traumatic.

The impact of trauma in our lives continues long after the event is over, and our minds and our bodies carry this danger mode that can be triggered at any time throughout the days, weeks, months, and years to come, long after the threat has passed.

We carry trauma with us in our physical and energetic bodies, and it can wreak havoc if it goes unattended. As distressing memories, thoughts, and emotions continue to invade and interrupt everyday life (consciously or subconsciously), they can strain mental health and have a significant effect on virtually every aspect of life.

A trauma response is the nervous system's way of keeping your body safe in situations that the body interprets as threatening due to past experiences. This can differ greatly from person to person. For some, it may be harder for them to build and maintain relationships and friendships because they struggle to trust people. Others who have suffered trauma struggle with daily functioning like the simple ability to hold down a job. Others have difficulty managing their emotions and can experience frequent panic attacks and/or depression. Sleep can be impacted. When traumatic experiences get retriggered, it makes it really challenging to cope with day-to-day living.

When learning about the impact of trauma, we need to understand the autonomic nervous system—the part of our nervous system that controls the functions that our bodies need to survive. These are processes you don't think about and that your brain manages while you're awake or asleep.

When we are faced with traumatic events, our bodies react by preparing us to respond. The fight-or-flight instinct is an automatic survival mechanism that kicks in without our having much control over it. Our hearts race, breathing becomes more difficult and shallower, and we may feel nausea, shaking, or dizziness. This is our body preparing itself to respond and protect us from the danger it senses.

The parasympathetic nervous system is the part of our autonomic nervous system that is responsible for the "rest-and-digest" body processes. Everything is functioning in a normal state of being.

The sympathetic nervous system kicks in during times of stress or perceived danger. This system is responsible for your body's "fight-or-flight" response. This is where our bodies go when we experience trauma of any kind.

I believe that when people experience trauma of any magnitude, they experience a type of soul injury that in effect disconnects them from their sense of self. When this happens, we enter a downward spiral of pain and suffering, bumbling around and searching for connection and meaning outside of ourselves when the real connection that needs to be made is within us.

We can spend our lifetimes suffering from the trauma and/or the limiting beliefs that were formed because of our experiences… or we can make a choice to begin a process of healing, to consciously decide to do the work required to reconnect with our true essence, our soul, our higher self, to feel whole again.

My own traumatic experiences, which I will be sharing in the upcoming pages, kept me in a perpetual pattern that was debilitating for me. I was lacking personal boundaries, over giving of myself, and I had an unhealthy compulsion to "rescue" people, all in a subconscious effort to prove my own worth. When I felt my giving was not being returned, it only deepened my pattern of feeling unworthy of receiving.

I discovered that having a mental awareness of these self-sabotaging behaviors was not enough to unwind it. These pains lived in my physical and emotional body, and I needed ways to help my body release its grip on me. This realization led me to learn about Somatic Experiences and Trauma Therapy. Both were game changers that enabled me to help heal myself and my clients who were keeping themselves victims in similar ways.

It is my hope that, by sharing these healing strategies, we will begin to break the cycle of dysfunction so future generations don't have to keep waiting to reach their fifties and sixties to start this process of unraveling and rebuilding. Let's stop the patterns of ancestral trauma and refrain from conveying our own unresolved wounds to our children. It begins with a willingness to be vulnerable enough to share our own stories, and to change the conversations away from shame and toward healing. The healing begins when we can experience the suffering to the fullest and move through it.

*The problem is to keep the
monkey mind from running
into all kinds of thoughts.*

-Lee Kuan Yew

LOST IN OUR THINKING BRAIN

Do you ever feel lost in your head?

Our patriarchal, male-dominated culture teaches us to value our thinking mind over listening to the wisdom of our emotional and energetic bodies. We are pushed to value rationality, science, and intellect, and this results in our bodies and emotions being disconnected or disembodied.

The reality is that most of us as women in the western world are not fully connecting with their own emotional and physical wisdom. We spend so much of our time with thoughts swirling repetitively in our busy minds and pushing our to-do list forward because we have been socialized to lead with our masculine "doing" energy.

We suffer early life experiences, attachment relationships, developmental trauma, gender roles, cultural norms, and many other factors that lead to our disconnection from our bodies. Societal narratives can create a challenging and undermining environment for women, both individually and collectively.

What we are not taught is that our bodies hold the key! Everything that has ever happened to us—every experience and every trauma—is stored in our subconscious mind and in our bodies, and those records define our sense of safety and/or danger. These are the experiences that form limiting beliefs and energetic blockages that hold us back from living life on our own terms.

When we push down our feelings, bury the traumatic memories, and fall victim to our limiting beliefs, the disconnection with our bodies only deepens. And, when we are out of balance in this way, we experience stress, anxiety, overwhelm, and burn-out.

When these spiraling patterns are left unattended, we may feel confusion and have difficulty making decisions. People who are disembodied often attempt to reach for alcohol or drugs to numb themselves, leading to addictive behaviors, challenging relationships, and physical and emotional dis-ease.

The good news is that we can learn to move through and eventually beyond painful experiences and repetitive patterns of behavior to be more embodied and express ourselves more freely.

Trauma is a fact of life.

It does not, however,

need to be a life sentence.

-Dr. Peter A. Levine

FEEL IT TO HEAL IT

Most of us who have experienced trauma or painful events in our lives spend years burying our pain and suffering under blankets of shame, all the while pretending that we are fine. But the truth is we are not always fine; those memories and experiences will continue to rear their ugly heads until we face them head-on with a vengeance.

The big question is, once we uncover and accept the fact that we have had traumatic experiences, what do with it?

How do we begin to heal from the trauma in our lives?

First it is important to understand that, when trauma happens, it's not something that just happens in the brain or in the mind. It happens in the body. The body then holds onto that fear and helplessness until it has a new experience that contradicts the trauma and results in a shift towards empowerment.

You can try to change your negative thoughts and overcome your limiting beliefs. You can try to understand where the trauma is rooted. But nothing will change until the changes happen in the body itself. Without changing the experience in the body, you cannot heal.

It is for this reason that I have invested in the study of somatics, or body-based methods for trauma healing, and found that we are all different and respond to different types of modalities and techniques or combinations of them.

Here are some of the somatic practices that trauma-informed practitioners use with clients, to name a few:

- Grounding & Centering
- Self-Touch
- Breath Work
- EMDR
- Emotional Freedom Technique
- Humming/Sound Healing
- Internal Family Systems
- Imagery & Movement
- Mindfulness/Meditation

When we work through our trauma with these practices, we start to lighten up, to rid ourselves of these heavy burdens, and to create space for healing. We break the patterns and limiting beliefs that hold us back. We begin to love ourselves. We return to our true nature. We reconnect to our deepest inner knowing to get back into balance and alignment. We see the world with new eyes and our relationships improve, as does our overall well-being.

There are some amazing teachers and authors out there, like Dr. Peter Levine, Bessel Van der Kolk, Pat Ogden, Ruby Gibson, Manuela Mischke-Reeds, and Richard Schwartz, to name a few, who were in my program educating on somatic experiencing approaches to trauma-informed care, including a deeper understanding of the body's relationship with social, environmental, developmental, relational, spiritual, and cultural wounding and healing.

I incorporate learnings from all of them in my own practice to offer a holistic framework for working with trauma from a body-centered perspective. And what I do know is that to heal, we need to allow ourselves to fully feel the pain we have suffered, every dark and dirty part of it, in our physical bodies (versus in our minds) so we can move through the emotions attached to the traumatic events.

This act of feeling into past trauma is not easy, but when we allow ourselves to fully experience our pain, we also feel the magnitude of the work that is going to be required to heal ourselves. This can be quite overwhelming in the beginning.

But in time, we begin to recognize that feeling pain can be productive and the only way to heal is to go through the suffering and put in the work required to find our truth. If we hold onto the pain, we remain victims and continue to suffer. When we work to heal trauma, we become capable of letting go of the role of being a victim and bring awareness to the present moment of taking responsibility for our own life.

When we live in our essential truth, we are making the conscious effort to feel the spectrum of our pain. We are living in it and through it. When we're willing to stick to this course, we find that facing our uncomfortable hidden dark parts of us is the only path to healing, peace, and wholeness. There is no avoiding the journey even though at times it seems so much easier to find an escape door.

Even in our darkest moments, when our foundations are shaken to the core, we can dig deep within and find the strength to do the work. The key is to sit in it, sit in sorrow and just feel everything without judgment. When we do that, we eventually find solace in the fact that it simply is... what it is.

Acceptance is one of the most important factors in the process of growth and healing. When we accept the way things are or the way events came to us, we can let go of the stressful behavior of reverting to that fight-or-flight mode.

In doing our healing work, we encounter the tools necessary to help us to let go, accept our life situation as it is, and find freedom.

This work of experiencing our grief is part of the human experience. Every one of us has weathered painful times, and in some ways, that shared human experience brings us together.

When we act in accordance with our deepest feelings, our lives become simpler. Instead of constantly choosing how to act or what to say, which inevitably results in more anxiety and self-doubt, there is always one choice: the choice that is true for us. The choice that we feel in our hearts.

The process I employ when working with clients who are going through this unraveling and rebuilding work includes the following phases:

- Name the painful event or traumatic experience(s)

- Claim those experiences as part of your story

- Recognize and feel where the pain lives in your body

- Move through the pain, rather than to avoid it

- Feel it to heal it

- Reframe the experience(s) to find the learnings

- Teach what you know and support others in their healing

The next time you are hurting, uncomfortable, or lonely, allow yourself to feel your pain fully. It's important that you feel as much of it as you can bear. Your pain is a necessary step on your journey towards healing. And remember that you are doing the best you can and, while it will not be easy, it will be worth it.

Healing is aligning with
your soul by releasing
any limiting beliefs that block
you from who you are and
what you are destined for.

-Unknown

SOMATIC PRACTICES FOR MOVING THROUGH TRAUMA

As a Certified Somatic Trauma Practitioner, I am a big believer in the power of implementing somatic practices and experiences, introduced by Dr. Peter Levine, for moving through Trauma and healing from it.

The word Soma means the physical body, and this work includes the assignment of body-based practices designed to help us suffering from traumatic experiences to:

- Reintegrate our minds and bodies to work toward a state of being where we can fully trust that we are safe in ourselves and in the world around us
- Calm our mind/body
- Appreciate the pleasure and joy of movement
- Improve our ability to self-regulate and be empowered
- Enhance our ability to connect with ourselves and others

Our bodies are like human libraries. We carry so much information within our vessels.

Somatic therapy may help you manage symptoms of trauma and chronic stress. Many of these somatic experiencing exercises can be done on your own, but if you are suffering from unresolved trauma, I recommend that you work with a trained somatic therapist.

I could write an entire second book on the different types of Somatic Practices but other experts like Dr. Peter Levine and Bessel Van der Kolk and Manuela Mischke-Reeds have already written them. Instead, I will share a few of the techniques I use regularly for myself and with my clients.

The first step is learning to self-regulate your emotions. Having the ability to regulate emotions can foster confidence, healthier relationships, and an overall sense of trust and ground-ed-ness. Regulating our emotions means that we can identify an emotion and manage our internal response to it. Many of us grow up not learning how to regulate our emotions, because we are encouraged to bury them. Rather than feel things, we tend to either dissociate, lash out, or numb ourselves from our emotions.

By practicing emotional regulation, we learn to actively choose how we want to respond to certain feelings rather than letting the emotions control us and our behavior. Here is how you can start practicing emotional regulation:

Notice the sensation in your body. Do you feel it in your chest? Your abdomen? Somewhere else in your body?

Name the emotion you're feeling. For example, instead of saying "I am not good enough," say "At this moment, I FEEL like I'm not good enough," using "I feel" rather than" I am."

Practice connecting to your breath and see if you can slow it down. This does not mean that the emotion will go away, but you will calm your nervous system by taking mindful, slow deep breaths.

Cultivate a self-soothing practice that works for you. This could be journaling, breathwork, dancing, calling a friend or having a warm bath. Find what works for you.

Within somatic therapy, self-regulation is about the nervous system and guiding yourself through your emotions so you can shift gears when they're leading you to feel distressed. Unresolved trauma may lead to dysregulation of the autonomic nervous system, meaning you're on high alert all the time. When someone is in a state of high alert, they may react to everyday stress in a way that's connected to their past trauma.

According to the somatic experiencing approach, talk therapy may not always be able to access this complex body process. Instead, working with your physical senses can help release and shift these patterns.

You can try some more of these easy at-home techniques to help you self-regulate.

Hug yourself. To do this, cross your right arm over your chest, placing your hand near your heart. Then, cross your left arm, placing your left hand on your right shoulder. According to Levine, this can make you feel contained, which may make you feel safe. Hold the hug for as long as you need. With your hand in a cupping position, tap your body all over, from your feet to your head. You can also try squeezing different parts of your body instead of tapping them. This will help you with grounding, but also help your body recognize your boundaries which can also give you a sense of being contained and safe.

Body Scan. Body scans are an "active meditation" that may help you relax. Here's how to practice body scanning:

1. Start by getting comfortable, possibly in a seated position. Close your eyes.

2. Focus on your lower body. Notice how your feet feel on the floor. Slowly, move your attention to your ankles, knees, thighs, and then pelvis. Identify temperature, pressure, tension, and any other sensations as you move up your body.

3. When you feel any tension, take a deep breath and exhale as you release it. When you feel the body part relax, you can move to the next one.

4. When you finish with your lower body, do the same with your upper body. Include focusing on some of your internal organs like your stomach, heart, and lungs.

Orient Yourself. When we experience trauma in our life, we can become triggered and go into a state of panic for "no reason." One of the ways to work with triggers is to ground yourself and orient yourself to the room around you.

It is important to know how to orient yourself to your body. Begin asking yourself these questions to increase your somatic, mind - body awareness.

- What does your posture feel like?

- Are you slumped, relaxed, or stiff?

- What is the natural rhythm of your heart rate? Is it racing, or is it slow?

- Where do you carry tension in your body right now? Do you have a knot in your stomach, neck or back pain, a headache, or tingling in your fingers? Is your eye twitching?

- What external or internal elements offer a sense of calm, be it a pet, a blanket, a place, or a memory of an experience with a loved one?

- What external stimuli trigger you—loud sounds, darkness at night, certain social interactions?

When you're healing from anxiety or trauma or are experiencing emotional triggers, it can be difficult to feel like your body is supporting you. However, everything we experience and all the sensations we feel in the body are forms of communication needing to be expressed. An important element in healing and getting stronger is inviting your body to help you, to be a resource so that learning to connect and communicate with your body can be a critical foundation for moving through trauma.

I read once that thinking of your triggers as a Google Translate can lead to knowing what is going on inside your body. I loved that visual because it's something we can all relate to in today's technology-dependent world.

To find relief from the pain we're experiencing, we want to notice what is happening, and then process and release the experience on a mind and body level.

Next time you feel triggered, practice the following somatic exercise to help you process through the experience and experience relief. Practicing this may also help you identify what is triggering your change in "homeostasis" so that you can have awareness for the future.

1. Notice. Inhale and exhale. Notice what you feel on, in, and around your body, including speed of breath, heart rate, and body temperature.

2. Think back to safety. Think back to a moment you felt most calm, safe, and most like yourself.

3. Identify at what point in time and/or in which part of your body you began experiencing discomfort or stress.

4. Replay the scenario from calm state to stressed state, in slow motion (as if watching a slow movie). Identify people, conversations, objects, or behaviors that may have made you stressed or uncomfortable or that stand out to you as you're replaying recent events.

5. Tune in to your body sensations as you recall the event(s) and slow down and notice if there is any shift in your body, a sensation of tingling, tensing, warming, numbing, or cooling in your chest, arms, legs, and face, or an overall change in body temperature.

6. Place your own healing hands on the area that has experienced a shift or change and breathe deeply. If it's an overall feeling, you can simply place your hands on your heart. Breathe.

By following these steps, when you feel triggered, you can help the body to process the somatic experience and release the tension. When you practice, notice what comes up for you—perhaps an image, sensation, awareness, or understanding that offers clarity to the situation. If nothing comes up, that's okay as well, because the act of simply slowing down and pacing your breath will be helpful.

I encourage you to practice some of these tools after you have an upsetting experience and allow your body to process the emotions and communications of your body. And remember your body holds SO MUCH WISDOM—you just need to learn to trust it.

When we are not fulfilling
our human potential,
we tend to struggle with our health,
our wealth, our relationships,
our creative fulfillment,
or even our spiritual connection.
Our struggles are here to help
us learn and grow,
not to keep us stuck in suffering.

-Karen Curry

YOUR HUMAN DESIGN

I believe we are intrinsically and energetically created to love ourselves, to operate from our true nature, to feel empowered and divinely guided to live our soul purpose.

The harsh reality is that our true nature often gets disrupted by experiences, trauma, and deep-seated limiting beliefs. Our conditioning is the culprit. We are flooded with messages every day about who we should be, how we should behave, and what is expected of us. Sadly, so many of us go about our lives being so out of alignment and losing sight of who we really are or how we are designed to be in this world.

When we forget who we are, we experience pain. But when we can learn to unravel and dissect, and better understand the root of our suffering, we can address it with greater awareness and on a much deeper level. This is why I talked earlier about feeling your way through your pain and suffering, allowing it to be your teacher and guide you through your healing journey. We can use it to propel us forward back into the light.

As part of this journey back to yourself, I recommend that you get in touch with your Human Design. We are all uniquely different, and it is so very important that each of us tap into our own innate gifts and traits so we can be the best versions of who we came here to be. By living in alignment with your true nature, your essence, you can live with more flow and ease.

Human Design is a modality that combines Eastern and Western astrology, the Chinese Ching, the Chakra System, Kabbalah, and Vedic philosophy, and is based on the division of personalities into five energy types that characterize how each of us exchanges energy with the world. It was originated by Alan Krakower, who published a book called The Human Design System under the pseudonym Ra Uru Hu in 1992.

I have found Human Design to be an incredibly meaningful way to learn more about your personality, emotions, and energy centers. It breaks down how you inherently make decisions and how you interact with the world and people in it.

Like astrology, the system is based on the time, date, and place of birth, but it goes beyond just looking at planetary alignment when you were born. It identifies the dominant chakras and provides an energetic blueprint for each individual.

The two most important aspects of someone's chart are 1) energy type, which is how you exert energy and exchange it with the people around you, and 2) authority, which explains how you make decisions.

Energy Types are the way you optimize your unique energy in all areas of life, such as relationships, work, sleep, digestion, and creativity, and ultimately how you can best create ease and flow in your life.

The five energy types are defined as Manifestors, Generators, Manifesting Generators, Projectors, and Reflectors. Each of these energy types comes with a specific description of when you're most productive, how you utilize opportunities (your Strategy), a sign that that suggests that you are living according to your human design (your Signature), and a particular feeling that comes up when you're not in tune with your energy type (your Not-Self Theme).

Your Authority in Human Design is your decision-making process. It's like your inner compass or intuition. Your strategy and authority work together to help you make decisions and move around in a way that's most aligned to your energetics.

As mentioned, Human Design charts go much deeper to explore each of the chakra's centers, whether they are defined, undefined, open or closed, etc., with numbers and connections between them that provide a significant amount of valuable information to help you better understand yourself.

There are many beautiful people out there offering Human Design Readings and Interpretations. You can even get the report run on your own by googling Human Design and then ask an expert to help you understand the report that gets generated. This modality is becoming increasingly popular for individuals as well for helping to improve group dynamics and relationships, including work teams and families.

Human Design is a must-have resource to have in your spiritual toolbox to help you understand how your body and mind are meant to run properly, and how to align yourself with others who can support your process in living out your authentic nature.

After all, the goal of our human experience is to break the patterns that keep us suffering and claim our joy.

How you love yourself
is how you teach
others to love you.

-Rupi Kuar

HOW ARE YOU LOVING YOURSELF?

I spend a great deal of time in my coaching practice talking with women about the importance of surrounding themselves in self-love and compassion. Self-love is a state of appreciation that you hold for yourself that grows from actions that support your physical, psychological, and spiritual growth. Self-love means having the highest regard for your own well-being and happiness, which means nurturing the relationship you have with yourself first, above everyone else.

Self-love doesn't come easy for most of us because we are programmed to put everyone else's needs ahead of our own. I'm here to remind you that putting yourself at the top of the list is not selfish—it's a vital ingredient to maintaining your health and wellness.

While self-love can look different for all of us, it encompasses being kind to yourself, forgiving yourself, losing the negative self-talk, trusting your intuition, and placing valuing on your own worth. This practice includes setting and maintaining healthy boundaries, prioritizing your own needs, and not settling for less than you deserve.

Self-love has everything to do with our ability to become more fully embodied... to embrace and inhabit ourselves in mind, body and spirit and return to our true essence. This conscious shift of really listening to our inner wisdom and honoring our needs is life changing and has a significant impact on overall well-being.

Let's face it: when we don't feel good about ourselves, we tend to look to other people to "make us happy" and seek external validation or approval from outside of ourselves. When we don't get the reassurance we are seeking, we often end up feeling weighed down by low vibrational emotions like disappointment and resentment.

Conversely, when we decide to love ourselves unconditionally, we take our happiness into our own hands. We learn to tune in and make time for what it is we need to be happy, healthy, and whole. When we make ourselves the #1 priority, we begin to see a positive ripple effect in our life and in our relationships. I know from experience that when I show up more authentically as myself, with a pure heart and good intentions for all, I am more present and mindful about the connections I'm making with myself and others.

When you learn to love yourself, you teach others how to love you. You exude a new sense of confidence of who you are and where you are going. You attract respect from those around you. You can maintain healthy boundaries and better protect your own energy. When you learn to love yourself, you find yourself living a more embodied and empowered life that is more in alignment with your dreams, desires, and core values.

*I reveal my wounds and how
I unraveled them so that others
may find the courage to embark on
their own path of growth and healing.*

-Jenn Gulbrand

OWNING
MY STORY

A SPIRITUAL PATH

This is the part where I remove my protective armor and reveal things about myself that I have kept deeply hidden for most of my time in this human experience. I am exposing all my edges in hope that we can begin to change the conversation.

When we are brave enough to be vulnerable and share our own stories with one another, we promote our own growth and healing as well as to help heal others who are suffering.

It is not my intention to harm anyone who I reference in my story. I believe you were all brought into my life for a reason and that our experiences together were designed to help me learn and grow. I hold only love and respect for each and every one of you. Thank you for being my teachers and for sharing and supporting my journey back to myself.

As a builder of supportive communities and safe, supportive spaces for healing, it may surprise my readers to learn that, for a better part of my life, I have felt unworthy, undeserving, disconnected, unseen, undervalued, misunderstood, and often like an impostor in my own life.

I lived nearly sixty years of my life carrying a heavily weighted subconscious belief that I was undeserving of love.

I have reflected on this deep wound for years, trying to determine when those dark seeds were first planted and how they became so rooted in my belief system. I have had many moments throughout my life when I felt like I did not belong anywhere at all—not on this planet or in this dimension.

The Akashic Records are said to be a library of souls where you can retrieve all the information about your past, present, and future lives. My records indicate that I have lived thousands of lives and that this may in fact be my last time here contained in a human body. I've been told by those who can read the records that I volunteered to come back one last time so I could finish the fullness of my desired experience in human forms. That's a lot of pressure my soul is putting on this energy body to finally "get it right."

I believe that I am an old soul who has been on many journeys. How do you know if you are an old soul?

- Have you faced trauma and hardships in this life?
- Are you an empath who can't stand the suffering of others?
- Are you intuitive in that you just "know things"?
- Do you feel as though you do not belong in this world?
- Do you prefer deep conversations to small talk?

If you answered yes to these questions, my guess is that you have also been here many times before.

I believe that my purpose in this lifetime is to tap into my own suffering to teach other women what I have learned... to convince you that YOU ARE ENOUGH just the way you are!

Stop shrinking and staying small and holding yourself back.

Show up in your BIGNESS and be seen and heard.

Radiate your light and be a beacon of beauty and light.

I have been told by more than one Seer/Spiritual Shaman that I am part of a Tribe of children brought to this dimension as part of a global healing manifestation to help uplift and heal the human heart. After years of diving into my own self-growth and healing, I understand that my life experiences were a catalyst to put me on this very trajectory—a search for a higher consciousness—so I could help lead others there.

Those personal soul experiences led me to the work I do today. Like so many light workers, my lives have been full of trauma and challenges to help prepare me for my soul's work in each life experience.

As a wounded healer, I had to learn that only through my own healing could I truly help other people heal, lifetime after lifetime after lifetime. And here I am.

This was not an easy journey, and I wanted to give up countless times... but it was my path to travel so I could learn, evolve, and ultimately support other women who are seeking to find their truth and uplevel their lives. For it is our own life experiences, our suffering and eventually our healing, that enable us to evolve together.

I am continually doing my own shadow work to shed these subconscious stories that held me back and prevented me from living my life in full alignment. Those deeply ingrained energetic and emotional blocks began the very moment I was born and took my first few breaths and followed me for most of my life until I could learn to name them and mindfully unravel them one at a time.

I want others on this consciousness path to know you are not alone. You are surrounded by angels and Spirit to guide you. You are simply having a human experience that will be full of opposing forces of light and dark. There is always someone ready, willing, and able to support you on your growth and healing journey. I will be first in line, because I see you. You are here for a reason. You just need to believe it and step into the light.

You define the moment,
or the moment defines you.

-Kevin Costner

DEFINING MOMENTS

We all have defining moments in our lives when our subconscious stories begin to take shape. For me, the most significant and debilitating belief system was formed on an early morning in late March of 1963, in Madison, Wisconsin, when my birth mother relinquished me for adoption.

I'm told I was very eager to be born and that my entrance into this realm came fast and furiously. My birth mother called a cab to the hospital in fear that she would not make it in time. Little did I know that this woman, who had carried me to term, had no plans to bring me back home with her.

I came out kicking and screaming, ready for a warm embrace that never came. She did not reach for me with a new mother's love, or gaze down at me in amazement of the little human she had just birthed. There was no physical touch or loving connection extended to me. Years later when we reunited, my birth mother shared that the only thing she was capable of at that moment was screaming in hysterics to have me removed from her hospital room in what she calls her emotional breakdown. As I took my first breaths as a newborn baby, I was alone.

My birth mother was a German immigrant who came to America after WWII. She never shared many details of her own early childhood experiences, but I'm certain she suffered a great deal of her own trauma growing up.

She worked as a hostess in a local restaurant and eventually engaged in an affair with the owner, a Sicilian-born chef. While this sounds romantic, he already had his own wife and six children at home. Apparently, many people in their social circles knew about the scandalous relationship. Sadly, their infidelities went on for years and caused a great deal of pain and suffering for both families.

When my birth mother became pregnant with me, my birth father, who was less than enthusiastic to learn about the illegitimate child he had on the way, made arrangements for my birth mother to travel to Milwaukee to have me aborted. For some reason unknown to me, she declined the opportunity to terminate the pregnancy and chose to carry me to term. It was not easy for her.

I believe that my birth mother's circumstances, at the time of my conception, left her feeling trapped and alone. She wore the scarlet letter for engaging in the affair and for carrying a married man's child. Her decision to surrender me for adoption was based on her desire to do what she felt was best for everyone involved. I know I was just an innocent baby who was born and had done nothing wrong, yet I carried the shame of my birth parent's indiscretions, and the pain it caused their families, with me throughout most of my life.

I hold only compassion in my heart for these two people who fell in love, for they carried their own ancestral-related burdens and traumatic life experiences. I trust that every one of us does the very best we can, in any given moment. The fact remains that I was abandoned as a newborn baby, and that shaped my belief system to feeling unworthy and undeserving of love. That story took root in my subconscious mind and would twist, turn, and entangle its way into the very core of my being for years to come.

We all have moments in our early childhood that leave a lasting impression on us. It's as if we are in a state of helpless hypnosis without any means to rationalize what is happening to and around us.

These experiences make up our subconscious wiring that can wreak havoc for our entire adult life when left unattended. It's only when we can identify and gently release those stories, and be willing to change the script, that the deep healing can begin.

After being relinquished for adoption, I entered the foster care system, where I remained for about two months until I was adopted. My forever family consisted of my parents, who were both teachers at the time, and their three young sons between the ages of six and nine. They all sat in church one Sunday when the pastor asked the congregation who could love another child. My parents walked out of the service that morning and looked at one another without having to speak about what they were both thinking... and the rest is history.

It appears as though my infant self was feeling helpless and fighting back against the forces that felt unfamiliar to me. The paradigm that emerged in my family history is that I was stubborn from the start. It is said that when I didn't get my way, I would hold my breath until I turned blue and passed out. The family pediatrician instructed my new parents to hold my head under cold water to snap me out of it, which they did. No judgment, but it's hard to understand why anyone would think this was a safe or reasonable way to manage a distraught baby. Perhaps what was needed was reassurance for the infant who was unable to orient and soothe herself? I am quite certain that my energy body still holds body-based trauma from this not-so-nurturing experience.

My mom was an intelligent, professional woman working full-time as an Elementary School Educator in our community. Our family was very proud of her professional accomplishments, as she earned many honors, including Wisconsin's Teacher of the Year. She competently raised four children and worked full-time, while still managing to volunteer at her church and in her community helping people in need. Her passion project was a home for moms and children needing protection from abusive relationships. She showered the shelter with food, clothing, and essentials to help support these women and their right to have a safe place to live. She always presented to the public with confidence, style, and grace, all while hiding her own insecurities and limiting beliefs that had formed during her childhood.

My mom described herself as a tall, gangly, and awkward teenager who never felt like she belonged. The limiting belief that formed for her was that her mother did not love her as much as she loved her younger sister, and she carried that belief with her throughout her life. Those feelings of not being good enough led her to bury her big emotions, and as a parent, she naturally taught her children to do the same.

She grew out of her awkward stage and into a very beautiful, poised young woman who was pursued by many male suitors. She met my tall, dark, and handsome dad at the University of Oshkosh, where they were both getting their teaching degrees. Their courtship was full of romance and took them on quite a fantastic journey together, culminating in nearly 74 years of marriage, four children, five grandchildren, and three great-grandchildren.

I do not doubt for one minute that my mother loved me. While I recall little in the way of physical touch or nurturing from her as a child, her love was ever present in so many other ways. Her greatest gift to me was exposing me to books and teaching me to read before I went to kindergarten. Reading and writing has always been a place of quiet retreat and reflection for me. She has everything to do with my appreciation for music and the theater. I have fond memories of the trips to Milwaukee to see musicals and ballets as a special thing we could do together. We fought like moms and daughters do throughout my teenage years. But, as I grew older, I came to better understand her and learned how to respond differently so I wouldn't trigger responses to her own unresolved wounds.

I love and appreciate my mother so very much because I genuinely empathize with her as a woman who felt unseen and unrecognized at times during her life. I see her so clearly as beautiful, brave, strong, resilient, talented, and compassionate. She was my role model for what it means to be a truly empowered woman. She has a loving, kind heart and lived her life in service to her family and to her community. I appreciate that my mom did her very best in every moment of every day to show up for her family despite her own painful life experiences.

My dad, a former high school science teacher and basketball coach turned businessman, always put his family's needs before his own. He was a man of great integrity and of few words, but when he spoke, people listened. There are countless stories of the ways in which he helped people who were struggling without ever taking credit or speaking of his own kindness and generosity.

He was the seventh of ten children growing up in a family with an absent, alcoholic father. Their mother was the primary caretaker for her children and worked as a welder on submarines to support her family. He was the first one to go to college, and he outlived all nine of his siblings until his passing at the ripe old age of 96. He had an impressive high school basketball career and, at seventeen, volunteered to serve in the US Navy in WWII, where he served as a radio operator on transport ships in the Pacific Ocean. His years of service afforded him the opportunity to attend the University of Oshkosh to earn a teaching degree, where he met my mother.

After graduating from college, Dad became a well revered high school biology teacher and boys basketball coach for 12 years. When I came into the picture, he left teaching and launched his own State Farm Insurance business to provide more financial stability for his growing family.

Throughout his professional career and in his personal life, my father exhibited the highest standards of personal character, integrity, devotion to family, and community, always believing that everyone deserves the opportunity to be treated fairly and have access to a good education. We have countless stories of how he took chances in his own life to help someone who was struggling in some way. He was a very humble man who never talked about his good deeds, but those people he helped along the way continue to come back, years later, to thank him for his acts of kindness that, in many cases, changed the course of their lives.

I spent my entire life trying to gain my father's approval. I would have given anything to hear him say that he was proud of me, but the words never came. I'm guessing nobody ever said those words to him either, because I know he carried his own unresolved childhood wounds of abandonment, poverty, and never feeling like he measured up to others (which could not have been further from the truth).

Dad always showed up for me when I needed him most, watching over me and my interests and reminding me to stop and smell the roses (quite literally). I know he just wanted to protect me, and my brothers, from being hurt as he had been in his lifetime. He used to say, "If you do not have your health, you have nothing at all," and those words remained with me and impacted how I lead my life today.

I adore my three brothers and hold them in my heart with so much gratitude. They welcomed me as their little baby sister with open arms, not thinking for a moment how my entrance onto the scene would mean less of everything for each of them. I recall so many sweet moments of them caring for me during the years, with their beautiful, sensitive hearts as well as many fun-filled memories throughout our adulthood as we raised our daughters together. They all grew up to be men of character and integrity, just like our dad. The love and respect I have for them runs deep.

I always felt as though I'd hit the jackpot when I was adopted by my family, because they are all good and honest people. As much as I love them, and know they love me, I never felt truly seen or understood at a soul level. Despite my parents' efforts to raise me as their own daughter, I often felt misplaced in their home, like a stranger navigating unfamiliar territory. I know now that the lack of connection I felt with my surroundings had everything to do with my own personal soul journey, and nothing to do with a lack of love coming my way.

My human design and personality were very out of alignment with their way of being. They were all introspective, quiet, and reflective thinkers who often kept their thoughts and feelings to themselves, while I was simply wired differently. It would have been so much easier if I had simply learned to model their character patterns to blend into the family dynamics, but something inside of me drove me to challenge my nature versus nurture. I believe that I was compelled to do whatever it took to differentiate from the tribe (subconsciously of course).

I naturally learned to shape-shift and portray myself with a confident, outgoing, and what was deemed an "overbearing" personality to hide my deep-rooted lack of self-worth. It was as if my personality characteristics were in some way forced to compete from a survival instinct. I find it fascinating that our young minds can do such complicated work behind the scenes of our consciousness.

There was a tendency in the family to avoid talking about challenges and to simply put on a brave face and operate from a "pull yourself up by your bootstraps" mentality. My parents both grew up during the Depression era, so lack and scarcity were prominent themes for them that they unwittingly passed down to us. They were both good, kind, hard-working people who did their very best to set worthy examples for their children.

Emotions were not something that were freely talked about in our home. I feel sadness around this fact, particularly for my brothers, because talking about feelings was especially frowned upon for them as boys. They were all very sensitive beings with real human emotions that may have been held in out of fear of being seen as weak. I understand now that our shared experiences growing up impacted the way we behaved as adults and raised our own families. This is how patterns and paradigms form for all of us and how family dynamics can cast shadows on who we are designed to be.

I always find it interesting to ask people to recall their earliest memories. I have two very different memories that come to mind when people ask this of me. The first memory is a happy one of being in my father's arms at church. Everyone was singing a hymn, while I was belting out a children's nursery rhyme at the top of my lungs to feel included. My dad's soft, brown eyes and the smirk on his face felt validating to me at that moment, as if he was saying it was okay to be me. It was a gentle, tender exchange that made me feel completely safe. What I did not know at that moment was that I would search for that same sense of validation from him and others for the rest of my life.

The first unhappy memory I recall was me as a toddler on a playground outside a daycare center. I had climbed up one or two rungs of the ladder on a monkey bar set to look across to the kids on the other side. An older boy climbed up the ladder behind me and refused to let me back down. I remember the frustration and fear building inside of me because I knew I was trapped with no way out. He bullied me into going across the monkey bars as the only way to escape. Of course, my little hands could not hold on and I fell to the ground, splitting the back of my head open. I blacked out, and recall returning to consciousness at the doctor's office screaming while having stitches sewn into the back of my skull. I am certain I had a near death experience that day, as the flashbacks are so vivid, like a recurring nightmare. That was my first lesson in what it felt like to experience a masculine attempt to crush me.

As I entered elementary school, my wild imagination often drew me into the quiet forest behind our neighborhood, where I could enjoy peace and solitude. It was there among the wise old pines and winding stream that I'd spend hours discovering the wonders of Mother Nature without a care in the world. I communed with mystical fairies who whispered secrets of the universe into my curious ears. I dreamed of discovering archaeological treasures from a time gone by. I pretended to be an archaeologist discovering Indian arrowheads and felt so naturally connected to Mother Earth, more grounded and peaceful when distanced from the realities of everyday life growing up in a small-minded town and neighborhood. An entire day could pass, in what felt like minutes, until I was called to return home. Those were magical moments of innocence and freedom that remain etched in my memories forever.

While my feet were planted in a physical world, I always felt like I was not "of this world. I felt different, like a foreigner in a land far away from my home. At some point, I discovered my connection to Source (the Divine) but can safely say that it was not something I understood at that point in my life.

I was seven years old when my maternal grandfather died from stomach cancer. I had grown very close to him and my grandmother after spending an entire summer with them while my mom had been hospitalized. I have such fond memories of walking a mile down the road from the house to the mailbox with my grandpa. I would listen intently to his colorful stories of a make-believe family named the Griswolds, who he had created to amuse me. I cherished my alone time with my grandparents, hunting for treasures in the woods, climbing trees, and watching Lawrence Welk after dinner with ice cream. My cousin's border collie would slowly crawl across the forbidden line of carpet, inch by inch, to snuggle with me and my grandpa, who pretended not to notice the dog at our feet.

When my grandfather became ill, I was not allowed to visit him and remember feeling completely dismissed by the adults who felt I was too young to say goodbye to this man I adored. It felt unfair to me, because I was old enough to know that I loved him and wanted to say goodbye. He came to me in my dreams the night of his departure from his physical body. Nobody believed me when I shared the details of our conversations, but still I sensed his presence very strongly. He remained with me in my dreams for quite a while after his passing, with frequent visits in the silence of the night. Eventually the connections faded away as I was made to feel that these were simply make-believe fantasies in my young, childish mind. But I knew in my heart they were real.

I also have beautiful memories of my maternal grandmother wrapping me in a warm towel after a bath and telling me stories of her childhood. I found pride in helping her feed her wheelchair-bound mother, who had suffered a stroke. My grandma would make me warm molasses cookies and open a can of apricots to share as a special treat. After my grandpa died, we developed an even closer relationship as I would go stay with her for sleep over visits. She lived well into her nineties and even made it to my wedding in a wheelchair in 1993. She was a beautiful, complicated, and hard-working woman ahead of her time in many ways. I was so fortunate to have two strong female role models in my life who overcame whatever roadblocks life threw their way.

Old Soul, there is a beautiful
thing inside you that is
thousands of years old.
Too old to be captured in poems.
Too old to be loved by everyone.
But loved so very deeply
by a chosen few.

-Nikita Gill

GROWING UP AN OUTSIDER

As I mentioned, I was the only daughter and the youngest child by six years to the three biological sons born into my parents' family. My brothers had all left the nest by the time I was twelve, so it was like being an only child once I hit middle school. It was a lonely and awkward time trying to navigate my way through it all without any siblings to guide me.

At that time, society expected girls to be quiet, submissive, and well-behaved. I never felt aligned with those expectations and questioned the inequities I observed around me. We went to church regularly and I was expected to attend Christian camps, teach Sunday school, and be "a good girl," but inside my soul was screaming in rejection of what felt oppressive.

Overtime, I learned to keep my progressive ideas to myself to avoid standing out. I felt disconnected from a male-dominated world that made little sense to me, because I did not understand the inequalities and why girls had different rules and expectations placed on them.

I put pressure on myself to be the perfect daughter for my mom and the accomplished athlete for my dad, but sadly, I never measured up in either department. I still feel the humility of my poor attempts to run track or get a home run to make my dad proud of my athleticism. The closest I got was competing in gymnastics and regrettably joining the middle cheerleading squad, where I was sentenced to the top of the pyramid due to my smaller size and stature. These were not my finest moments.

I did my best to assimilate into the world around me as a late-blooming adolescent. There were difficult moments, like being mocked for having rather large, prominent, so-called "Marty Feldman bug eyes" and desperately trying to find my people. I found most of the girls to be catty and mean, and it was almost easier for me to become invisible than to follow the crowd. It wasn't until the 7th grade talent show, when I sang in public for the first time and won first prize for my performance of the Diana Ross hit "Theme from 'Mahogany'," that I began to find my voice. I find it curious now when I reflect on the lyrics and why they resonated with me.

Do you know where you're going to?

Do you like the things that life is showing you?

Where are you going to? Do you know?

As I grew older and found the courage to speak up with my opposing and often outside-of-the-box points of view, I was branded for being bossy and overbearing by my family. This paradigm, created by those closest to me, hurt me very much, because it felt stifling and oppressive. As painful as that time was for me, I recognize it was only the beginning of my soul's journey to finding my own way in this lifetime of lessons.

I'm uncertain of the exact moment when I lost sight of my feminine power and shut down my spiritual connection. It's more likely that I had never been properly introduced to the concept of the sacred feminine and the divine at all. Like so many young women growing up in the Sixties and Seventies, I was put in my place as a female in a male-dominated society—sit pretty and be quiet.

High school was no picnic. Is it for anyone? I received a less than quality education in a small Midwestern, conservative town where the environment was less than inspiring. I avoided associating myself with any of the cliques that were forming around me. Girls were cruel and boys were immature, and it seemed as though everyone I knew was all about making weekend plans for the next beer keg party. I rebelled against social standards to be what was considered popular and quit the cheerleading squad to become a musical theater nerd. That pretty much ended any chance I had at winning a popularity contest, but I was okay with that.

I didn't know it at the time, but I was clearly an Empath who felt the emotions of everyone around me. I experienced the suffering of the socially awkward kids who struggled for acceptance, and I consciously distanced myself from those bullies responsible for causing people pain. My parents, who were hands-off, let me dance to the beat of my own drum with little guidance provided to me, outside of communicating house rules that I was expected to follow. Looking back, I wish they had provided more direction to me, as I felt like I was often left to figure things out on my own.

Singing and acting in high school musical theater performances elevated my confidence to the point where I felt that I belonged to a community of sorts. My choral director was my mentor and perhaps the only teacher with whom I ever felt a meaningful connection. I consistently received high rankings in music competitions around the state, singing Italian arias and immersing myself in all the school plays and musicals, playing the leading roles in The Music Man, Oklahoma!, and Camelot. But here again, I did not always feel comfortable being in the limelight based on my feelings of inadequacy and comparing myself to my contemporaries.

As if I was not awkward enough, I worked after school at a high-end clothing store at the local mall and was asked to be a high school representative of Seifert's "Girl on the Porch," sporting painfully preppy clothing in the newspaper. Perhaps some of my contemporaries remember the Farrah hairstyles and monogram sweaters. I was basically selling Pendleton wool suits to middle-aged women looking to brand themselves with a certain social status. While I did not love the job, I did learn a thing or two about the psychology of sales.

One of the best experiences I had in high school was being selected to participate in a week-long model United Nations at the University of Madison. It was so freeing to get out of my small town and that locked-in feeling of small-mindedness. I was excited to be immersed in the energy of so many students I did not know and who had no preconceived perceptions of me.

Graduation was anticlimactic. I really didn't resonate with any of my high school friends and gravitated to hanging out with some of my brother's older college age friends for social engagement. I had received a scholarship to a small, prestigious music college to study voice performance and acting, but opted to attend the University of Wisconsin-Madison instead. I believe I went to lose myself in the crowd because I preferred that to putting my energy into standing out. Madison was a party town where the emphasis was more on beer and fraternity fests than on academics. I stumbled my way through four years, all the while trying to establish an identity of my own. I regret not taking the opportunity for a higher education more seriously.

You don't just grieve once.
You grieve as many times as
you come into contact with the loss.
The void can resurface in endless ways,
bringing you closer to both
the pain and your healing.

-Vienna Pharoan

GRIEF AND FATHERLY LOVE

Grief is one of those taboo topics that people avoid in conversation like the plague. That does not change the fact that death is a reality of being human. We all experience loss of loved ones in our lifetime, so why do we have such a difficult time talking about death and dying and what can we do about it?

Grief is an emotional suffering we feel when something or someone we love is taken away from us. When we lose someone we love, everything changes. No matter how old you are or how much time you've had to prepare, it can shake you to the very core. It can be overwhelming, and those of us who experience loss may have a wide range of thoughts and unexpected emotions that make it difficult to sleep, eat, think clearly, or function at all.

Another pivotal moment in my life occurred when my dad's body was preparing to leave this earth just a few months shy of his 97th birthday. I received so many blessings in knowing and loving this man who taught by example to always do the right thing. I am truly grateful to have been present for his transition, surrounding him with only the purest intentions of light and love. In the end, that is all there is... love.

I felt honored and blessed to be back home in Wisconsin with my family during Dad's final week of transition. I was alone in the room with him when he took his last breath. I whispered to him that it was okay to let go. I encouraged him to plant his wildflower garden and fill it with birds. He finally let go and journeyed home.

While helping my family support Dad's transition to spirit was a gift, it came wrapped up with an overwhelming sense of loss and sadness. I thought I had adequately prepared my heart for this part of his journey after receiving news of his terminal cancer diagnosis six months earlier. I made several trips back to Wisconsin to spend time being fully present with him, saying all the things I wanted to say, expressing my gratitude, and learning all I could about his life here on earth.

When the time came to say our goodbyes to this mountain of a man, I felt a gentle and peaceful release for him. What I had not anticipated was the fog I'd find myself wandering through in the days, weeks, and months following his death. I had lost loved ones before, but it was as if I was experiencing grief for the very first time.

I believe that when we pass to spirit, we do not leave our loved ones behind. People are made of energy, and energy cannot be created or destroyed—it simply changes states. I hold onto the idea that when we die, we exchange energy with our surroundings and our soul—our true essence—continues until the end of time. Knowing this to be my truth, I look for my dad's energy in the sky, the trees, the birds, and the flowers and find solace in knowing his presence is all around us.

Grief and loss are very personal, and each of us experiences it differently. Whatever you have been through or may be going through as it relates to the loss of a loved one, my advice is to feel all the feels without embarrassment, shame, or regret. Allow the pain to surface and the tears to flow and hold loving space for healing. Accept the support being offered and talk about it with those who will listen. Life is beautiful and intense and full of give and take. Be here now and look for the blessings in having loved so deeply.

In my commitment to be a truth teller in this book, about my own suffering, I am here to share a different kind of painful life experience relating to my dad's passing—one I have not spoken of until now, as it is something I am still processing. My dad did not acknowledge my presence even once during that entire week that I had come home to Wisconsin to help support his transition.

Even the first two days when he was still lucid, sitting up and able to eat, there was no acknowledgement of my being there for him. No mention of my name or words directed to me from my dad. I brushed it off at first, because I knew he was in so much physical pain and felt paralyzed by fear of what was happening to him. My primary intention was to be there to support him on a peaceful transition, but it hurt me very much and underscored my story of being unseen.

I watched as he asked for my three brothers by name, as well as my nieces, and they each came, one by one, as I sat beside him and listened as he spoke words of wisdom to each of them. He even mentioned my daughter, who was traveling in Eastern Europe, and expressed his concern for her safety. I waited, but he had no words for me.

By day three, he could no longer get out of bed. I stayed near his side, in love and appreciation, kissing his forehead and holding his withered hands that had once palmed a basketball with ease. I had become a hospice nurse without training, responsible for dispensing morphine every two hours to keep him as comfortable as possible, sponging his parched mouth, gently massaging his swollen legs and feet, changing his bedding, and wiping him clean. My dad's inability to acknowledge me holding that space for him deepened the tragedy of losing him.

In the days that followed, I rationalized his inability to acknowledge me with the explanation that he was embarrassed that his only daughter had to witness his rapid decline as he lay there so vulnerable, weak, and suffering. But the painful life experience that got stuck in my body is that my dad did not make a connection with me because I was not important to him. This is yet another story that I am working to unravel and nurture the child-like part of me who feels unworthy and unlovable.

In the end, it doesn't matter that my dad did not see me, because there is nothing he could have done to make me love him any less. They say that the greater the love, the more intense the grief can be for us to endure. So that in itself is a beautiful gift.

I am still grieving the loss of my dad, who was my hero and my safe place to land. This experience of grief and loss, coupled with feeling dismissed by him, only underscores the point that we are all carrying unresolved trauma and, as parents, we pass those wounds onto our own children.

I have forgiven my parents for not being able to fully understand me, because they did not have the capacity to. They were raising me through their own struggles, worries, pains, and fears. Forgiveness is such an important part of healing. I hope my own daughter will grant me the same grace someday, for I know I have unintentionally passed some of my own unresolved trauma onto her.

If we're ever going to
heal in our community,
we have to heal the perpetrators
and heal the survivors,
or else it's just a continuous cycle.

-Tarana Burke

ME TOO

Feeling unseen most of my life only drove me to work harder to stand out and succeed in my professional career. I am what is considered petite in stature and realize now that I had spent a better part of my young life trying to overcompensate for my smaller frame. My attempts to present a bold exterior and larger-than-life personality were most certainly my subconscious in the driver's seat attempting to overcome the fact that I felt so unseen and insignificant on the inside.

Long before the MeToo Movement was even a thing, I put up with a lot of inappropriate and sexist behaviors just to be taken seriously by the men who felt compelled to demonstrate their dominance over me. I could share many stories of sexual harassment in the workplace when male colleagues and superiors put me in vulnerable positions with male clients with absolutely no regard to the way it may have compromised my comfort and safety.

One boss comes to mind almost immediately. I looked up to him as a successful businessperson and mentor in the medical education company outside of Chicago. He was a very large man who used his size and stature to intimidate others. He continually promoted men into the higher-level management positions, over women, regardless of their capabilities and work ethic. He had a pattern of hiring young, attractive women in the role of project managers to interact with his pharmaceutical company's clients, who were typically male. I commuted from the city to the suburbs to the office and often went into the office on weekends because I was ambitious and single. One Saturday, I walked in to find this boss in a compromising position with one of his female employees. It was a very awkward and unpleasant experience, as she was under his desk at the time. Let's just say I stopped going into work over the weekends. It makes me sad to recall how powerless he had made me and other women in the company feel in that less than supportive work environment.

I recall being on a business trip to New York with him when we were scheduled to have dinner meeting with a high-powered cardiologist from California. My boss knew that this physician made me feel uncomfortable, as he had made his personal interest in me known on several occasions. We met in the lobby, and, out of the blue, my boss said that he felt ill and had to go back to his room. He basically ordered me to go out to dinner alone with this physician. I did not know at the time that I had the power to say no and went reluctantly, only to endure one of the most uncomfortable nights of my life.

The experience left me feeling confused and frustrated, and hurt that my employer would knowingly put me in a situation where I would feel unsafe and unprotected alone in the city at night with this touchy-feely client. I was a young, female employee for whom he should have felt some responsibility. Looking back at his reckless behaviors, I understand that he too must have been suffering his own wounds and unable to see the disrespect and disregard he was showing toward me and other female colleagues.

Fortunately, over time, I found enough courage to remove myself from the less than supportive conditions that this boss continued to create in the company for the women who worked there. Those experiences left me with emotional scars from being discriminated against based on my gender and more limiting beliefs about not being seen or valued for my capabilities.

I was determined to be respected for my contributions and to earn my seat at the table on my own merits. While it was far from easy, I spent years working my way through the imbalance of power, one glass ceiling at a time. Within just a few years, I advanced from an entry level Associate Project Manager role in Chicago to the VP of Strategic Operations at a sister company in Boston, answering only to the partners.

The harassment I received in my last role as someone's employee was from a female partner in the Boston firm. She was a bright, charismatic woman whose vibrant energy attracted great talent to her company. I was really drawn to her and felt very fortunate to have been given an opportunity to work with and learn from her. My work ethic and drive to succeed was strong. Every day I would commute into Boston on the first train to arrive at my desk by 7 a.m. Most nights, I worked until 7 p.m. I loved the industry, the clients, and the teams I got to manage.

Eventually, the charm of the job began to wear off, as this boss made my life a living hell. She manipulated me, and others, in ways I had never seen before. She knew I was a dedicated employee who consistently worked 12-hour days. She would put off meeting with me all day long and then call me into her office as I was walking out the door to catch the last train home out of the city. I never understood the motivation behind it. I suppose it made her feel powerful to have control over me in this way. I began to notice dramatic inconsistencies in her mood and behaviors, and eventually the communications became strained with her. She would give me one set of directions one day and then completely change her tune the next time we met, implying that I had not done what she had asked of me. This was never the case, because I took my job quite seriously. Looking back with the life experience I have all these years later, I can see that I was being gaslighted long before I even knew what that term meant.

I watched so many brilliant colleagues come and go from her company because the work/life balance of her employees was not something she valued. I believe this woman, as dynamic and successful as she was, may have been suffering from her own demons and unresolved traumas. I have learned that every experience we have in life holds a lesson in it. This work experience and unhealthy environment taught me how not to treat employees, who are the most important asset of any business. When I left her company in 1998, I knew I was ready to start my own business and do things differently.

LOSS AND RELATIONSHIPS

We all have a good breakup story, and here is mine. Upon returning to Madison from overseas where I had spent a semester abroad my junior year in college, I suffered a painful breakup with my boyfriend of three years. He was a really great person, but he suffered an alcohol addiction problem with multiple DUIs and repeated loss of driving license privileges during our time together. It happened more than once, and he resorted to getting to and from the beer parties on his bike. Our relationship starting in freshman year had begun as they all do, full of fun and physical attraction. But over time, things began to go downhill. He was a party guy who would disappear overnight with no explanation of where he'd been or what he'd been doing. I found myself feeling more drained than supported in the relationship.

I applied to travel abroad to London for the first semester of my junior year. We had been feeling disconnected for months, and yet he was clearly uncomfortable with my decision to take off to a foreign country without him. My experiences abroad those next few months were mostly positive. It was exciting traveling to new places with an entirely new group of people. There was a lot of exploring of my freedom being so far from home with no one to hold reign over me. Although I do shudder to think of some of the risky situations I put myself in during that time as we feel so immortal in our young twenties... I surely had a team of Angels looking after me and protecting me.

Toward the end of my semester abroad, the college boy-friend traveled to meet me and a friend for a visit to Greece, where I had hopes for a reconnection and a new start. But upon returning to Madison, I learned he had been seeing another woman while we had been apart. While it felt like betrayal to me at the time, I believe that parts of me were relieved to be free of the constant worrying about his mental and physical health and well-being. Our separation, however, added even more subconscious wiring and beliefs that people I cared about would eventually end up leaving me because of my perceived inadequacies and lack of self-worth. I am happy to see, all these years later, that he eventually found stability and bal-ance in his second marriage and appears to have a beautiful extended family and love surrounding him.

The realization that I have come to is that most of my longer-term adult relationships were with men with substance abuse problems of different magnitudes, be it alcohol or drugs. I had apparently created a story in my head that I was here to save people to prove my worthiness, and this mindset has plagued me my entire adult life. My own limiting beliefs and low self-worth impacted my relationships and professional ex-perience as an emerging adult and followed me for the next 30+ years. They were all beautiful men with both light and dark inside of them, and the experiences I shared with each of them brought me valuable lessons.

After graduating from the UW in 1985, I moved to Bos-ton to experience complete separation and independence from almost everyone I knew, and I never lived in Wisconsin again. Thankfully, I had my brother, with whom I had always felt a close connection. He was so kind to take me in to sleep on his couch until I found my own housing. I took some classes at the Harvard Extension School and worked some odd jobs in and around Boston and Harvard Square—everything from going canvassing for MASSPIRG, a local grassroots organization, seeking donations to save our planet, to working in a clothing store in Harvard Square, to doing admin work in real estate offices and advertising agencies. I took some Harvard Extension classes as well to keep my mind fresh and learning. I was drawn to the energy of the city and the open-mindedness of the East Coast vibe and met so many interesting people along the way.

Here comes another truth bomb... when I was 24 and living in Cambridge in a rent-controlled apartment with six other people, I became pregnant. I was not ready to have a child, especially one conceived in the circumstances I'm about to share, and I had an abortion. This is the first time I am saying these words out loud (or in print) because very few people know about that low point in my life. I've lived with the heavy burden of guilt and shame of it for years and kept my pain locked deeply inside the secret vault.

My boyfriend of two years had seen me out at a club one night with a male colleague from work. He showed up hours later to my apartment and stormed into my room in a jealous rage. He was drunk and high, extremely angry, and determined to prove his possession of me and my body. Half asleep, I had no time to respond to the aggression, let alone consent or secure the appropriate birth control precautions. The rest is a blur and a nightmare that has haunted me ever since.

Here again, someone I cared about ended up hurting me. More limiting beliefs on top of the piles of debris already residing in my energy body.

Years later, I have had to wade through the healing from the fact that this man, who I loved and trusted, had raped me. I am sure he would not see it that way because, after all, we were in a relationship. But in my experience, the event was violent and non-consensual. The months that followed were very painful and the beginning of the end for us. I still hold a great deal of love and compassion for this man. He was another struggling soul carrying his own childhood wounds, battling depression and numbing himself with self-sabotaging. Again, this wonderful person, who I cared deeply about, found his way to a loving relationship and balanced family life. The learning here is that all of us need to find ourselves in safe, supportive spaces where we are allowed to feel our pain and move to a place of healing.

I spent years hiding the secret of that traumatic experience and somehow blaming myself for being responsible for what happened. I told no one about what I had been through except one girlfriend, who was kind enough to take me to the abortion clinic to endure one of the worst days of my life. I felt so alone and empty returning home that day, full of shame with no one to console me. I took on 100% of the responsibility for yet another burden that was not mine to carry alone and spent the next 15 years believing my inability to have my own biological children was in some way a punishment for somehow inviting the attack and subsequently having the abortion. I suffered in silence, further fueling the limiting belief that I was unworthy of love and happiness and that in some way I deserved what had happened to me.

Not long after, I was quite literally swept off my feet by my future husband, a charming musician/bass player, 13 years my senior. With kind eyes and a soft, sensitive way about him, he too had a sensitivity about him, having been raised by an alcoholic, abusive father. Do you sense a pattern here?

We had an intense physical attraction to one another almost immediately despite our mutual agreement to keeping the relationship platonic. He had recently left a long-term relationship and was in avoidance mode, and I too was recovering from my recent separation. In spite of our resistance, the universe kept drawing us together. He lived a typical musician's life, working a delivery job by day to pay the bills and playing gigs by night in an industry fraught with substance abuse. I knew it was not a healthy setting for me, yet I was drawn to him in a way I had never been to anyone before. I was young and free, in a place and time to explore and embrace all the possibilities. I knew I was in trouble when I continued to make him the priority in my social calendar above the other men pursuing me romantically at the time.

After a year of ups and downs in that relationship and what felt like a dead-end job, I moved back to the Midwest. I was not seeing much long-term potential in the relationship or in my career. I was under the delusion that I missed home, but I think I was just running toward something more familiar.

My brother came to my rescue again and drove me and all my belongings in my leased Mazda all the way back to Chicago, where I began yet another new chapter. I had another supportive older brother who lived in Lake Forest with his wife at the time. He helped me secure a tiny apartment on the second floor of the house in which they lived below. I used to go down to their apartment after their dinner to eat their leftovers. They were so kind to me at a time in my life when I felt a bit lost and disconnected.

My newly found independence in Chicago began to re-energize me. My masculine energy tendencies led the way, as I secured an entry-level job in a medical education company on the North Shore and worked around the clock to prove myself. Over the next three years, I climbed the corporate ladder despite gender inequalities and way too many rounds of sexual harassment, which I shared earlier. Always searching to belong, I cultivated friendships, some fleeting and others lasting the test of time, and clumsily found my way through it all.

As part of my trauma healing work, I have had to come to terms with the fact that I was also the victim of a date rape drug while living alone in a suburb of Chicago. I had met a very charismatic young man who had been flirting with me around town for months. I should have listened to my instincts that there was something "off" about him. I learned he had been in a very serious boating accident a few years earlier, while on a drunken binge with a group of friends, and one of them had died tragically. We hung out a few times as friends. One night, after having dinner together, we returned to my apartment to grab a beer and talk. The next thing I remember is waking up on my bedroom floor several hours later and remembering absolutely nothing, and he was gone. I'm certain he had put something in my one beer, because I have no memory of what had happened. I shudder to think about the fact that I was violated without conscious consent. I never saw him again. More shame, self-loathing, and disgust to be piled on my already low self-image. The script kept replaying in my mind that, once again, I must have done something wrong to attract yet another act of violence and betrayal.

While going about my life in Chicago, I spent four years in a long-distance relationship with the charming bass player back in Boston. No matter what I did to try and distract myself from him, the force of our connection was too strong.

We took the plunge in 1993 and got married. I was 30 and he was 43, and my parents expressed their concern about the age difference, which of course did not stop me from moving forward with my Aries determination.

It was a small, simple, fairy tale wedding at the American Club in Kohler, Wisconsin, surrounded only by the close friends and family who were invited to celebrate with us. Those first few years of my marriage were magical. I was certain I'd found my soulmate, a partner who would love and adore me forever. We enjoyed living in a vibrant city like Chicago among so many friends, really resonating with the energy of city living. I worked in medical education while he wrote music in his makeshift studio in the basement of our two-flat apartment rental. We did not have much in the way of material possessions. Life was simple and beautiful, and we were in love.

In 1996, we moved back to a suburb of Boston, where I had been recruited to serve as the VP of a sales training company. We bought a beautiful home in a quiet cul-de-sac in his hometown and began living the dream. I commuted into the city, while he created his music in the studio we'd built together in our walk-out basement. We were still very happy.

Two years later, I co-founded my own sales training company in the life sciences industry and located the headquarters near our home, attaching my self-worth to being a smart, successful, savvy entrepreneur. We built a company from the ground up, and I always say it was attending a real-life business school without the master's program certification. I did love the role of visionary and creating something from scratch. More on that later.

It was during that time that I sought out and reconnected with members of my original birth family back in the Midwest, something I had put off for years out of fear of hurting my adoptive parents. The journey to finding my biological roots was full of pain.

My half-sister on my birth mother's side, 13 years my senior, was extremely accepting of me when I turned back up again in their lives. But it became clear, over time, that she had endured a great deal of her own pain growing up as a latchkey kid. Her mother, my birth mother, was always at work and had little time for mothering. She was dealing with her own unresolved childhood wounds relating to abandonment by her absent father and what she experienced as emotional neglect by her mother. At times, I felt so guilty that I had somehow escaped the difficult times she had living with a single working mom. That was again my own belief system kicking in and burying me in suffering and shame. This was not my burden to carry, but I took it on anyway.

The six half-siblings on my birth father's side all had their own reactions to my attempt to reconnect with them through the years. I had reached out by letter to the oldest brother, a special person who was so kind to me and whose wife had a lot to do with our finally reuniting. Some of the siblings were accepting and open, while others were angry and accusatory. I do not fault any of them for the way they responded, as they too had suffered from being children of a father who was unfaithful to their mother and a less than calm presence in their lives.

The stories they shared about their memories of their father/my birth father and his affair with my birth mother are soul crushing. They are not my stories to share here in detail, but they suffered greatly. While I know intellectually that I was just a baby born because of their indiscretions, I carried the weight of their pain on top of my own grief, shame, and a sense of responsibility for what had happened to them. The piles of rocks on my back just kept multiplying.

To make matters worse, my own adoptive family did not fully support my desire to reconnect with my birth family in the way I had hoped they would. They did not seem to want to understand that my decision to search for my roots had nothing to do with my love for them and everything to do with my need to fill in some missing pieces of my own identity. My mom had always told me she would be there for me when the time came to search for and reunite with my biological family. But, when the time did come, it was painful. She really struggled with my decision to meet my birth mother, and while I understand that her response came from her own insecurities, it only added to my feelings of guilt, shame, and responsibility for causing pain to someone I loved.

My dad's response was quite hurtful, as well as he accused me of being foolish to accept this woman who had given me away once before saying, "If she didn't want you back then, why would she want you now?" I know that he was just being protective of my mother's feelings, but the general lack of understanding and support from family at that time added even more baggage on top of the limiting beliefs I held about myself being undeserving of love and connection.

The full details of my adoption story are not necessary to expand upon here. The point is that this was another dark cloud that hung over my life, leaving me feeling rejected, ashamed, and not good enough. I was forever suspended in between two families, not fully belonging to either, and these dynamics only further supported the subconscious stories of my unworthiness and lack of belonging.

Adoption is the most
intentional process on Earth.

-Jody Cantrell Dyer

MOTHERHOOD MY WAY

What does one who feels undeserving of love and belonging do with those feelings of inadequacy and lack of connection, you may ask? You guessed it! She tries to whip up a family of her own to recreate what is missing in her life.

Five years into my marriage, I felt the maternal instinct kick in and began yearning for a child to complete our family. Despite my husband's lack of enthusiasm to add the title of Dad to his resume, due to his own childhood trauma of physical and mental abuse at the hands of his father, he succumbed to my wishes, and we launched into the adventure. Unfortunately, over the course of three years, I suffered three devastating miscarriages between 12 and 14 weeks into each pregnancy. I can still feel the agony in my body of setting up a baby nursery and taking it down again repeatedly... it felt like a crappy Groundhog Day, over and over again.

My lost baby girls were named Isabella, Sophia, and Grace. In those two years, I had seen enough heartbreak and loss for one lifetime, but it did not stop me from trying again. In July of 2001, I became pregnant with twin boys.

I felt so hopeful as we passed the first trimester mark for the first time and sailed through the amniocentesis procedure with flying colors. The nursery had been lovingly designed for this round, this time with little-boy treasures and an original wall mural painted in anticipation of their arrival. I loved being pregnant and the feeling of life growing inside me.

Then we were hit as a nation with the horrific 9/11 tragedy. My father-in-law had also passed during this timeframe. I did my best to stay positive, awaiting the March birth of our beautiful twin boys, Enzo and Maxx. Sadly, on the first of November, I woke up unknowing of the tragedy that was about to knock me down to my knees yet again. I had felt off all day at work, taking a walk for lunch and getting a prenatal massage, all the while not knowing that I was in premature labor. I remember having tortilla soup for dinner and retiring early to bed with what I thought was heartburn. As I lay there that night, I intuitively knew something was not right. I remember stroking my belly and talking to my boys inside my womb, telling them I loved them and to stay safe.

I woke up at midnight in excruciating pain and my water broke moments later. We rushed to the hospital 30 miles away and the rest is a blur. My OB-GYN, who had been through all my former miscarriages with me, was not on call, and the male attending physician was lacking in bedside manner and empathy. He told me my labor was too progressed to stop it and that my boys' lungs were not developed enough to survive outside the womb. I spent the next 18 hours in mental and physical agony waiting for their birth, knowing they would not be returning home with us.

Being in a state of shock, at one point, I left my physical body and recall being elevated above everyone in the room. I was looking down at myself lying on the table in the surgical room, viewing it all in a slow motion black and white movie. My husband's head bowed over me on the right in horror at what he was witnessing. Two nurses stood on the left side near my feet beside the doctor, tears rolling down their cheeks. The doctor handed me my dying babies, one at a time. I was dead inside and had to make the choice in that instant to stay or go with them. I replay that moment in my mind repeatedly. My boys were so small and beautiful, and saying goodbye to them that morning, cracked my heart in a way that could never again be repaired.

The days, weeks, and months that followed were swallowed up in an earth-shattering grief. I was empty and void of any kind of feeling. My husband could not be there for me in the way I needed him to be. He too was suffering loss of children he had not even realized he had wanted. I tried to get us into couples therapy, but he resisted. To make matters worse, if that's even possible, it became painfully clear that my partner in life no longer desired me physically and that intimacy was no longer possible for the two of us.

Imagine my having to come to terms with the fact that my partner could not bear to touch me after watching my body fail at the birth of our twin sons. Not only had I lost my children, but I had lost my dignity, my self-respect, and my perceived value as a woman. Talk about defining moments.

I had hoped that, in time, we would both heal and find our way back to one another. Never did I imagine that the loss of our boys would break our physical relationship into a million little pieces, but it did.

You may wonder how I managed through this pain. Did I seek out support? Did I tap into my sacred divine feminine energy and allow myself to grieve? To feel? To release? To heal?

No, I soldiered on with my masculine energy in overdrive. I took the blame and more shame and piled it up on top of the other mountain of sludge I had sold myself over the years. I believed that for some reason I deserved everything being handed to me and had no choice but to buckle up and endure it.

As a typical Aries, I was not going to let anything stop me from fulfilling my desire to nurture and mother a child. I pushed hard for adoption, and my husband finally waved the white flag in surrender. We sought out an international adoption program and chose the Guatemala program. We also signed up for the dual domestic inter-racial program, because we honestly did not care about the color of the child's skin. Perhaps I felt in some unconscious way that bringing a new child into our grieving family would somehow help us heal as a couple.

On February 8, 2002, while we were in the middle of our intensive home study program, we were called by the agency with an opportunity to switch to the Russia program. It was explained that there were a few children in an orphanage outside of Moscow who had been in the system longer than usual and who needed adoptive families who were ready and willing to travel at a moment's notice and within weeks. We were all in!

We raced to Wellesley to meet our social worker, who handed us the first photograph of our new baby girl. She had the most beautiful, dark brown, expressive eyes. I fell in love in a way I never knew was possible. I spent the next few months preparing her nursery with a John Lennon Imagine theme. Night after night, I sat in the soft yellow rocker watching the video we had of her, waiting anxiously for the call giving us permission to travel. I was determined to be with her in time to celebrate her first birthday together that March.

The universe had other plans for us. Delays and political circumstances had closed the adoption related travel to Russia, and her birthday came and it went. I was in agony all through April and May thinking of the conditions she was living in and not being able to get to her. We finally got the call to travel in early June and had 36 hours to pack and get our visas flown to us from California. They arrived at 3 a.m. the day we were set to travel (no stress there).

The 28-day adventure in Moscow was just that… an adventure. We almost lost our papers at the Moscow airport the day we arrived due to the confusion and lack of language. We had been required to hire and pay an interpreter and a driver, to keep us safe on our daily trips from the hotel in Moscow to the orphanage 45 minutes outside of the city. I remain forever grateful to both of them for guiding us through such unfamiliar territory and keeping us safe.

I will never forget the first time we walked into Orphanage #21. My heart was pounding outside of my chest as we were guided down the long, bleak hallways that smelled like a combination of cabbage and urine. We were met by two physicians in the office, two older women who ran the children's home. One was tall, thin, and stern, and the other was short, stocky, and very approachable. We came to love them both over the next month as we witnessed their dedication to the children who lived there. We walked down the corridor past rooms filled with children's toys and wondered why they were void of any children.

We reached the end of the hallway and followed our guide up a set of concrete stairs. When we got to the top, I knew instinctively that our daughter was just through a set of closed doors. We were greeted by two rough-looking caretakers who were in charge of caring for this pod of children. I remember thinking they looked so tired and beaten down from life. We listened intently as our interpreter explained who we were and why we were here... to meet our beautiful baby girl.

I began to take in the faces of the toddlers, all between 12 and 15 months old, lying around the room with jumpers made from old-fashioned and stiff fabrics. They were all pale with sunken eyes from what I assumed was from being undernourished. Some of these children gazed up at us, while others remained rocking themselves in the corners looking lost and vacant. And then I saw her. She turned toward us from across the room with a big, captivating smile that seemed to say, "What took you so long?" I had to hold myself back from running to her because the women who were in charge made it clear without even speaking that I was not to move until told to do so.

I waited anxiously for one of the women to dress her and remember feeling disturbed by how rough the caretaker was handling this fragile baby girl of mine. This beautiful, precious girl just took it in stride, staring at us from the changing table and smiling that smile as if she knew we were there for her. The woman hesitated and finally handed this precious little being to me, sizing me up and down as if she were trying to evaluate my worthiness. In that instant, my entire whole world changed when my arms wrapped around this small baby bird.

Everything and everyone else faded away. I knew I was here to love this little human and expose her all the wonderful joys of life that she so deserved. There was no doubt in my mind that we were meant to be together, and I was her mother.

We went to court two days later and stood there being measured up by complete strangers and having no idea what was being said to us or about us (Russian is not a language you can learn easily). Most of the other families who had traveled with us had returned to the US to wait for permission to come back for their children, but we had chosen to stay and wait it out. There was no way I was leaving my daughter there alone. Life has a way of repeating patterns, and I would never be the one responsible for a baby being abandoned by her mother.

We were only allowed to visit the children's home for one to two hours at a time each day. The staff looked at us cross-eyed when we asked to take our girl outside to get some sun and fresh air into her. They would bundle her up in four layers of clothing and hats, even though it was warm summer weather in June. We took her outside every day to this funny little playground and found it astounding that we were always the only family out there. We would walk and talk and cradle her in our arms as we sang her Beatles songs. I would kiss her hands to make her laugh and she showed me very early on that she liked to be held very tightly. She would wrap her little arms around mine and pull them in closer to her body. It took her a little longer to warm up to my husband, because she had never seen a man before and was fearful at first. They soon bonded over his baseball hat, so we bought her one of her own.

Each day, when our visiting time was up, we were forced

to leave her there alone in those less than nurturing conditions. The ride back to the hotel was always very difficult for me because I just wanted to kidnap her and save her. Our hosts were very good about making us feel comfortable and welcome and keeping me occupied. We took in a lot of Moscow, marveling at the incredible architecture and history, enjoying an international piano competition and a performance at the Bolshoi Ballet, and visiting colorful markets. I wanted to soak in as much as possible of our daughter's culture.

The hurdles we had to jump through to become parents were shocking and exhausting. We had brought an extra suitcase full of medicines and diapers for the orphanage but also had to bribe officials with money and gifts to get the appropriate papers processed in a "timely" manner. The disparity in that country between the classes was unsettling and very eye-opening.

On June 24th, 2002, we were finally given permission to take our daughter out of the children's home to remain with us. We still celebrate this as our Got-Each-Other Day. We spent another week at the Marriott Tverskaya Hotel getting to know one another on a whole new level—experiencing her first bath, first book, the first time she saw herself in a mirror (she couldn't stop giggling), and her first cozy nap between the two of us. It was an unusual yet beautiful process of becoming parents—and the most incredible month of my life.

We returned home to Massachusetts on July 2nd greeted by a banner made by the neighborhood children and a house full of baby gifts left by friends and family. I will never forget those moments of introducing her to her new room and the way in which she embraced it all as if it were meant to be. This was the beginning of my role as Mother, and I wanted nothing more than to give this special girl the world. I didn't know I could love another human this much!

I would be lying if I didn't admit my frustration over the fact that my self-employed musician husband had the luxury of staying home and caring for our new daughter, while I had to return to work every day to support our family. I know it was not easy for him either, as his day-to-day routine had changed dramatically, moving from playing bass grooves in his home studio to changing diapers and listening to nursery rhymes. I would rush home at the end of each day in time for dinner and tubby time for those few hours leading up to reading and bedtime. But deep down, I regretted every minute that I was not able to be a stay-at-home Mom with her. I knew in my gut that I was missing out on the opportunity to nurture and bond with my new baby. It was a tough time for me.

My husband, who is a good man, rose to the occasion and leaned into his new role. Sadly, our physical relationship had not improved despite our new family structure. We did our very best to manage our nontraditional roles, with me as financial provider and him carting our daughter to Baby and Me music movement classes. He continued to reject therapy because he did not acknowledge that we had a problem.

The awkward truth that I never share is that I spent the next 22 years in a marriage with no physical touch or affection, while the rest of the world looked on, remarking on how lucky I was to be married to this kind and caring man. The dynamics behind our closed doors were not what they seemed on the surface. Yes, he was (and is) a very good person and I love him, but, like most of us, he suffered from his own unresolved trauma. He is on his own path of healing, and part of that growth is being okay with my writing about our experiences together. I have worked very hard over the years to forgive and release myself and my husband for the distance that grew between us. But the truth is that I subconsciously felt abandoned all over again, just like that newborn infant who was left alone and afraid.

Even though I felt desperately lonely in my marriage, I was 100% committed to staying together, because that is how I was raised. The day we got married, my father had said, "This is forever, you guys," and I took those vows seriously. Rather than taking the necessary actions to get the help I needed, I kept powering on with my masculine pattern of "doing" and providing for our family. I continued with these unhealthy patterns only further feeding into the subconscious beliefs about my lack of worthiness.

What I understand now, but didn't then, is that our early conditioning can greatly affect our adult relationships. The more we become aware of our behavioral patterns, the better we can heal from the wounds we have carried with us from our early lives. If our early relationships neglected our emotional or physical needs, we may feel unworthy or broken and mirror that toward other people, especially those closest to us. I regret not having more self-awareness and knowledge of my own wounds all those years ago. Perhaps things could have been different in my own marriage.

I share this very raw personal story of loss and what felt

like rejection to illustrate what can happen when we deny our-selves the right to feel and express our pain and fail to secure the support we need to heal from it. Rather than opening up, honoring those soft and vulnerable parts of me during times of tragedy, and asking for help, I reverted to my masculine tendencies and fell back into roles of loyal caretaker and finan-cial provider for my family. I operated a 35-person company by day and did my best Mom impression at night and on the weekends.

I know that I was short on patience most of the time. The interpersonal dynamics with my business partner were deplet-ing my energy. My fight-or-flight stress response was activated often. The burden of sole responsibility for our family's security and well-being was a lot of weight to carry. I felt as though it was up to me to keep a roof over our head and provide enrich-ing educational opportunities for our daughter.

I worked tirelessly to earn enough to get her into the best private schools and enrichment programs so she could be ex-posed to all the things I had not had while growing up. My husband managed the home and meal-related responsibilities, but he had a very low stress existence in comparison to mine. It was my perspective that he found it easier to become our daughter's friend and leave all the boundary setting to me. I now understand that he was suffering his own unresolved childhood trauma and had rejected any positions of authority.

I over-compensated my intended role of nurturer and be-came a helicopter mom. In my attempt to be a superwoman providing for my family and holding up the ceiling, I was craving the opportunity to nurture a loving mother/daughter bond. But it all backfired on me and drove my daughter even closer to my husband and further away from me. I became what they deemed controlling when all I wanted to do was take care of the people I loved.

My biggest regret and greatest sadness in all of this is the impact that our broken marriage had on our beautiful daughter. She had already suffered enough trauma before we became a family, and the very last thing I ever wanted was for her to be anything but happy, healthy, and whole. The tension between my husband and me, and the pressures I felt to hold the roof up over our heads, caused her pain and suffering. And now, as an adult, she is on her own healing journey back to wellness.

Subconscious limiting beliefs of abandonment and unworthiness kept me imprisoned and unhappy for a very long time and most definitely impacted my ability to be the wife and mother I wanted to be. I was always judging myself and shaming myself for not meeting my own expectations in life, especially in the role I so wanted to fill of being a good Mom.

Once again, I felt like an unseen, undervalued outsider looking into a life I did not recognize. It felt nothing like what I had imagined for myself. And there I was again, alone and feeling like an outsider most of the time. I never felt truly appreciated or valued by my husband and daughter—but here is the a-ha moment! The problem with that skewed perspective was that I was seeking validation from outside myself versus finding it from within myself.

Nobody did this to me... these were choices leading up to this point in my life. I was locked in my own subconscious stories and patterns of thinking—and the subsequently patterns of behaving.

I operated from masculine energies "doing" (and not feeling) rather than mindfully accessing more innate feminine energies of "being" and allowing myself to feel and receive what I needed most, which was love, validation, and support.

After decades of stifling my own pain and suffering relating to my limiting beliefs about myself and the world, I gradually began to wake up. I made a commitment to do the work to heal from my own trauma and to stop projecting blame on others around me for contributing to my sadness and despair. I reconnected to my own inner wisdom and started listening to my spiritual guides. I began to flex my own intuitive muscles and re-engaged with my gifts as a spiritual coach and healer. This shift led me back to myself slowly.

I learned to love myself. I learned to forgive myself and others. I rediscovered my own value and stopped looking outside of myself to find my worth. I slowly unraveled all the limiting beliefs and subconscious stories that had blocked my progress for so many years. I practiced the art of detachment—separating myself from these roles and responsibilities that put everyone else's needs before my own. I began to look inward for the purest of love for myself versus the old patterns that had me relying on it coming from others around me.

Once I began to work through the past trauma and learn to release it, everything began to change. I found myself backing off of the "go, go, go" and easing more into the flow.

I'm not going to pretend that any of this has been easy. It was raw and ugly, and I fell out of my practice and out of alignment time and time again. I had to work very hard to learn to let go of people in my life who were not ready to evolve with me. I had to consciously stop trying to have conversations with people who were unwilling to change. I had to practice forgiveness for myself and for the people in my life. I set myself free from the chains that had bound me for so long.

I had to show up differently, or in some cases, not at all. I had to learn that I am not responsible for anyone else's happiness. In time, my relationships began to improve, particularly those with my husband and daughter, who had suffered their own trauma in childhood and in life. I learned to release most of the expectations I held for them and for myself and, in some ways, detached from outcomes. We all did, and continue to do, the work to heal our individual wounds so we could improve our dynamics together and begin again. It was very raw, painful, and exhausting, but also so worth it, as communications began to improve remarkably and I felt less and less alone.

You may wonder: why I am exposing my deepest darkest secrets to the world? Because I believe that we are all wounded by the things that happen to us, and we can either let them paralyze us or we can feel them, move through them, heal from them, and live forward from a place of love.

The scars we all endure run deep and can handicap us for a better part of our lives. But when we learn to face the darkness, do the soul-searching work, and show up more fully embodied as ourselves, only then can we begin our healing journey and find our way back into alignment.

*Truly great friends
are hard to find,
difficult to leave,
and impossible to forget.*

-G. Randolf

YOU'VE GOT A FRIEND IN ME

Losing my close friend, Joann, to cancer when she was only 52 years old shook me in a way I had never been shaken before. When she shared her stage IV non-smoking lung cancer diagnosis with me, I felt the earth crack open beneath my feet and everything looked and felt different in an instant. I was reminded that we only have today and need to seize every moment. Conversations with Jo, during her battle, inspired me to stop living small and start following my heart. I was determined to find a way to recalibrate and get back on course with the life I was designed to be living.

I had met Joann when our daughters started pre-school together. We bonded almost immediately over having adopted our daughters. She became the sister I never had—always there for me, from the beginning. Jo had a beautiful, magnetic smile, an infectious laugh, a nurturing spirit, and a heart like no other. It didn't take long before we felt like family—celebrating milestone birthdays, important holidays, and creating lasting memories that are now even more precious. Memories that I will hold in my heart forever.

What strikes me most is how easy and naturally our friendship formed—more than likely based on a shared vision of hope and promise we both held for our young daughters. We had many heartfelt talks over the years about life, usually centering around motherhood and how we wanted our girls to grow up to be strong, confident, young women who felt empowered and capable of achieving big dreams. Her two daughters were always Jo's priority. She set a best-in-class example for them with her grace, courage, and generosity toward others. In spite of the unbearable pain I continue to feel in her absence, all these years later, I find comfort in knowing that her radiant spirit lives on in her girls and that they will always know how much she loved them.

When we first learned of her cancer, I asked Jo what she desired most, other than the obvious need for more time with those she loved. She told me she wished to take her family back to China and for her girls to experience their birthplaces. Being an adoptive mother myself, this resonated so deeply with me. I'm so grateful that, with the help of an amazing tribe of people in our community, we launched a fundraising campaign and raised enough support to make her dream come true. The pictures of their family trip to China, and the beaming smiles on their faces while they experienced the journey together, will forever be etched in my mind.

Jo lived her life authentically and was one of the most genuine people I have ever met. Her honesty and valuable insight are missed by so many of us who sought out her advice and support.

We spoke frequently in the months following her diagnosis about the importance of being mindful and living every moment being true to yourself and not sweating the small stuff, because our time on this earth is so brief.

Breathing—something so simple that we all take for granted—became such a struggle for Jo because of the disease invading her body. I found myself so often wishing I could breathe for her and find a way to take her pain away. It was this realization, coupled with reminder of the importance of living life to the fullest, that gave me the courage to take a leap of faith and launch my heart-centered mission to create a space for women to practice self-care and lift one another up in support and sisterhood—the way my friend did for me time and time again.

My one regret is that, in my love for her, I was unable to face the harsh reality of her impending death as it drew nearer. It was unbearable for me to accept, and I desperately wanted more time. I didn't want to believe her time was coming to an end and can only hope she forgave me for being weak when she needed me to be strong.

Joann, while you left us far too soon. Thank you for your gift of friendship and for making me a better person for knowing and loving you. Until we meet again... I will remember you.

Focus on making choices
to lead your life that
aligns with your core values
in the most purposeful way possible.

-Roy T. Bennett

THE TIME I FELL OUT
OF ALIGNMENT

When I had finally kicked and crawled my way up to the top of that wobbly ladder, my first wave of entrepreneurial energy struck me. I was over this game of having crazy bosses who held their perceived power over me and set out to find the financial backing I needed to launch my own sales training company, one that would put its people first. I wrote a business plan, sought out a business partner, and secured a financial investor, and within a matter of months, became the co-founder of a sales training company in 1998.

Because of my own insecurities and limiting beliefs, I felt I needed someone with the business connections to launch the business. I had sought out a specific woman with whom I had worked quite collaboratively with in the past and invited her to be my partner. I chose her not because of our similarities, but because I felt her strengths and talents complemented mine and made for a powerful leadership team.

My first mistake was being too insecure and convincing myself that I needed a partner to make the dream come true. Hindsight is 20/20, but I gave away too much control when I agreed to an equal partnership because I didn't feel confident enough to do it on my own. My second mistake was not going to a bank and getting my own business loan. I simply lacked the confidence.

Again, feeling insecure and not quite good enough, we signed with a parent company and financial backer out of

New York and gave up 90% ownership in exchange for administrative and financial backing. I spent the next 21 years applying hard work and grit to building the business up to being a premier provider in the life sciences training space. Six years into the endeavor, we got some backbone and bought the company back from the financial partner, becoming an independent, women-owned business.

I found tremendous value serving in a leadership role, building, and supporting a team's professional development, and providing best-in-class customer service to our clients. I was able to afford nice things for my family, take them on trips, put my daughter into the best private schools.... but something was always missing for me. I knew that working in that industry was not my true calling.

I realize now, looking back over the years, that when I had faced adversity in my lifetime, I tended to lean into my masculine energies and not honor my own divine feminine. Those were times when I had started to behave in ways that I did not like or understand. I resisted, rather than allowing and accepting things for what they were. I felt out of alignment most of the time but continued pushing forward in my masculine doing energy, spending my days in constant conflict with my business partner and feeling stuck.

I pushed for what I thought was right instead of allowing things to flow. I frequently compromised my own personal and ethical values to protect my employees and their families, who were always my number one priority.

I still hold a great deal of respect for my business partner and don't see a need to share the details of our professional relationship or its decline. Let's just say there were a series of circumstances involving other people who came between us, and that severely disrupted our flow as friends and colleagues. Those experiences broke our trust with one another, and we were unable to recover. The last five years were extremely damaging to my physical and emotional health. I was suffering from dis-ease on a regular basis. I knew it was time to get out no matter how hard it would be for me, my employees, and my family.

We sold the business for far less than it was worth after 21 years, paid off the bank debt we had incurred, and parted ways with little to show for our years of labor. I vowed to never enter a business partnership arrangement or work for someone else again. The freedom I felt in walking away from that part of my professional life, and most of the people in it, was life changing. It did not mean I didn't care, but that closing that chapter was what was necessary for my own survival and re-birthing. I let it go and began focusing my time and energy on putting something more meaningful into the world.

Finding your soul's purpose
for being here can be
a lifetime adventure,
so enjoy the ride and the
learning that comes with it.

-Jenn Gulbrand

CORPORATE DROPOUT GONE GODDESS

I am grateful for all the personal and professional experiences I endured during those 21 years owning and operating my sales training business. I was genuinely proud of our success. The business mission was worthy, it fed my family and supported my employees and their families, but the role was not feeding my soul. I was lacking a community of like-hearted people, and I felt uninspired.

As mentioned, I was drowning in a toxic business partnership and often compromised my own values to keep the peace. I felt the call to break free from the corporate framework but, like so many of us, fell victim to negative self-talk and allowed those limiting beliefs formed in early childhood to prevent me from moving forward.

Do I have anything unique to offer?

Can I risk walking away from financial security to follow my heart?

What if my dream isn't well received by others?

And then, as I shared previously, when my friend was diagnosed with stage IV lung cancer, everything changed for me, propelling me forward to create a different future.

In 2016, I bravely stepped out of my comfort zone and created the SheBreathes Balance Women's Collaborative with the intention to create and hold space for women to practice self-care, experience sisterhood, and be supported by a tribe of like-minded women. It was at that moment that I began vibrating on a higher frequency, helping to change lives and living a more authentic and soul-filled life.

Three years later, I put fear aside again and took another leap of faith. I released ownership of my sales training business and completely let go of what no longer served me. I stepped into solopreneurship as a Spiritual Well-Being Coach, Trauma Informed Embodiment Practitioner, Energy Worker, and Sound Healer, dedicated to helping other women reconnect and rise.

Two weeks before the global COVID pandemic hit, I signed a lease to expand our physical space to create WeBreathe Wellness, an inclusive retreat center for he/she/they/they/us/we to experience growth and healing. My timing may not have been ideally suited for expansion, but I stayed the course. I know now that I was being divinely guided to create and hold space for healing that would be even more necessary after two years of the COVID global pandemic.

My spiritual awakening has been painful at times, but I know in my heart that Source was driving me to take actions that were for my highest good so I could use be of service to others. I continue to put faith over fear and move forward with courage.

Finally listening to my inner voice and leaning into my feminine energy of allowing myself to sit in my feelings was what led to my healing and resulted in dynamic shifts unfolding in my life. While on this transformational journey, I discovered my deep passion for empowering women to rise and support one another in sisterhood and community. But my own rising did not occur until I had endured and responded to a great deal of pain and suffering. I had to wade my way through a lot of thick, dark muck to finally put energy toward my rising. We can do hard things!!

No Mud, No Lotus!

We can always learn something
from our experiences,
even the painful ones.
Once we have an experience,
and learn the lesson we
were meant to learn,
we can release the suffering
and move forward
to a place of healing.

-Jenn Gulbrand

LESSONS IN LIVING FORWARD

NOT SO GREAT... EXPECTATIONS

I have collected many valuable lessons in my life experiences that I share in the following chapters in hope that they will help you to find your own truth and brilliance.

Perhaps the most significant learning of all is that, as William Shakespeare said, "Expectations are the root of all heartache."

Expectations refer to the beliefs that you hold for the outcomes of events or of other people. The simple truth is that our expectations can lead to major disappointment when reality does not match up to what we had hoped someone would do or how a situation will unfold.

Some of the common signs that you might hold expectations include anticipating a certain outcome, holding a vision in your mind of how things will play out, or having a set idea of what you want or need from another person.

Pain comes when our reality doesn't match our expectations. When expectations are not met, it can lead to feelings of disappointment, frustration, and anger. We need to be careful not to become so attached to our expectations.

Due to our social conditioning, most of us expect to have achieved certain milestones in life by a certain age. We expect to be married, have a family, climb the career ladder, or reach the top in a specific way within a set amount of time. When reality doesn't live up to that road map, we suffer. We blame our circumstances, ourselves, and other people for our disappointment.

The truth is that life doesn't owe you anything—so maybe we can reduce our suffering when we stop expecting it to play out a certain way. Maybe we can find more ease, and less resistance, in allowing and accepting what comes our way. Maybe when we can stop having expectations, we will stop being disappointed.

Now let's consider our relationships and the expectations we hold of other people. We expect other people to be kind, respectful, and trustworthy, but that is not always the case, is it?

Have you ever thought about the fact that many of our relationships with other people are transactional in nature? Transactional relationships tend to include a focus on the other person's contributions to the relationship. There may be a sense of keeping score, with both people concerned about "getting" rather than simply "giving." Expectations may be clearly defined, or they may be unspoken and simply assumed by one or both parties, but they are more often than not based on contributions of one or more parties. There is an expectation of reciprocity and needs where both parties expect to receive something in return for their investment, whether they are conscious of that or not.

Think about your relationships for a moment. Are they based on self-benefits? Do you focus on what you are getting out of it? Is there an unspoken commitment of equal giving and getting?

Now think of a time when a relationship of yours has fallen apart. Did one of the people in that relationship fail to keep their end of the deal? Did one of you feel let down and disappointed in the other? We all enter into these transactional relationships based on expectations without doing so consciously, and we have all suffered when those "contracts" are broken.

What if we created relationships based on authentic connection versus having them be transactional and based on expectations? What would happen if the emphasis in our relationships was placed on love, trust, care, and connection?

I wonder if the key to improving our relationships is to enter them more consciously, being mindful of the other person's needs and feelings, and committing to giving without expecting anything in return. In doing so, we would allow ourselves to learn new things, grow, and truly connect with one another without expectation or perceived outcomes.

When we can practice living our life free from expectations, we begin to be more fully in the present moment. We turn our attention inward, instead of focusing on all the external circumstances and judgments. Our lives become focused on acceptance, gratitude, and love. We stop fighting things that are out of our control and focus our power on what we can control: our own mindset, emotions, and actions. Learning how to be happy without expectations means realizing that fulfillment comes from within. This realization has transformed my life.

We learn our belief systems
as very little children,
and then we move through
life creating experiences
to match our beliefs.
Look back in your own
life and notice how often
you have gone through
the same experience.

-Louise Hay

LOSE THE LIMITING BELIEFS

I spent far too many years trying to prove my value by rescuing people and assuming responsibility for everyone else's happiness. Then, when those people I attempted to nurture did not acknowledge, express gratitude for, or validate my efforts in return, I felt invisible, under-appreciated, and misunderstood. I was waiting to be seen, yet no one recognized me. I felt invisible and created the story in my head that the people in my life didn't value or care about me.

Then I began to identify and unravel my limiting beliefs, one layer at a time. I worked to release the unhealthy habit of rescuing "lost souls" because it was not my job to save them. I learned that detaching from those we love and allowing them to lead their own lives was the best kind of love. I stopped looking outside myself for validation and began looking internally. I practiced self-love and acceptance and connected more deeply to my higher self.

I reactivated my sacred feminine goddess energy and showed up in new, softer, less masculine ways that were more reflective of this deeper truth. I empowered myself to elevate every area of my life. Now it's your turn. Because feminine energy has a lot to do with receiving, you may unknowingly block that which is ready to come to you simply by being in disharmony with the divine feminine.

I have grown to understand that my subconscious limiting beliefs of abandonment and unworthiness—being unlovable and undeserving—kept me imprisoned for most of my life.

On the outside, I was viewed as a high-energy extrovert, a social person with ambition and exceptional leadership skills. But the truth is that on the inside, I never felt like I fit in anywhere or belonged to anyone.

I was always working on overdrive, led by masculine energies, trying to push forward and to prove myself-by being the best in every role I played—daughter, sister, friend, employee, wife, mom, employer... The truth is that I had been setting extremely unrealistic expectations for myself and for the people in my life.

My biggest disappointment was never feeling truly appreciated or valued by people to whom I gave myself in service. I continued throughout most of my adulthood to feel deeply hurt and wounded when my family called me "overbearing" and "bossy" and or commented that my "pace is too much" when I was attempting to help or do something kind for another human. I got lost in my own drama about everyone else's lack of gratitude when I repeatedly gave of myself to them and then felt as if they did not recognize or appreciate my giving nature.

I have countless stories of what I experienced in my subconscious mind about how friends, family, boyfriends, and colleagues had mistreated me—all based on my belief system that I was unworthy and unlovable, so people would naturally continue to disappoint me, betray me, and abandon me.

My self-inflicted limiting blockages and patterns were so clear.

- I stayed in a toxic business partnership for years.
- I avoided dealing with problems in a dysfunctional marriage for years.
- I passed my own unresolved trauma onto my daughter.
- I stayed in unhealthy, one-sided friendships for years.
- I convinced myself I was doing the honorable thing by putting others' needs before my own and remaining in patterns and behaviors that did not serve me.

I saw myself as a victim—but NEWSFLASH! That was the farthest thing from the truth. This was all my own stuff! Other people's actions were NOT the real cause of my suffering. I was doing that all on my own by falling victim to my own deep-rooted limiting beliefs that, no matter what I did, I would not measure up. I was operating from a belief system that I was unlovable and fearful of being alone again—just like that newborn baby girl left in the hospital moments after her birth. See how this works?

It is through your body
that you realize you are a
spark of divinity.

-B.K.S. Iyengar

BE EMBODIED AND EMPOWERED

On top of all of those limiting beliefs that had attached themselves to my subconscious and held me back for most of my life, I was suffering from a perpetual state of disembodiment—a disconnection from my physical body. That's right—I was too in my head, which is where most of us tend to operate from.

I was emotionally, physically, and spiritually depleted. I suffered from debilitating insomnia. I was not setting or maintaining healthy boundaries and not protecting my own sacred energy. I lived in fear of disappointing everyone around me and completely lost that connection with self. This state of disembodiment is a very dangerous place to be.

I was caught up in a male energy dominant culture that places value on the ability to think, reason, make decisions, and get sh*t done. I admit to being all about navigating my way down my to-do list, but I'm here to share how I have spent a lifetime learning that there is much more to being human than making things happen!

In my current coaching practice, I work with women every day on the concept of conscious embodiment. I use trauma-informed somatic experience practices to reconnect clients back to themselves, to help them to become more fully embodied, physically, and emotionally, so they can move forward by "being" in their own body and in the world.

Embodiment, at its essence, means inhabiting more of ourselves. Emotional embodiment is the ability to feel our emotions with sensitivity so that we can better embrace and express them in empowered ways. Physical embodiment means making a real connection with our body and treating it as a temple where we've been gifted to live. Simply put, when your body talks, you need to listen!

As we addressed earlier, most of us as women are not fully connecting with our own emotional and physical wisdom. We get stuck in our heads and lead with our masculine "doing" energy.

When we are just in our heads, we become disembodied, a state in which we are disconnected and unaware of our emotional and physical sensations. We shut down our body's natural gift to feel things and express itself. When we are in a disembodied state, we may feel confusion, have difficulty making decisions, or hold beliefs that we're stuck or not good enough. We may eat our emotions, reach for sugar or alcohol, or break our own personal boundaries because, when we are disconnected from ourselves, we tend to feel disconnected from others too.

We need to learn the practice of dropping from our heads back down to our hearts—to our being energy—and let that inner knowing guide us back from a state of "go" to one of "flow." By doing this, we learn to listen to our emotional and physical body and respond with what it needs.

This is not a practice that comes overnight. It takes years of introspection, conscious awareness, spiritual self-development, and a commitment to breaking down learned thoughts and behaviors to master the art of embodiment—of being fully connected with yourself in body, mind, and spirit.

I'm excited to share some of my own life experiences in an effort to speak to women everywhere who may be struggling from this phenomenon of being disembodied and just going through the motions of life in your head.... until you hit a wall and BAM! It becomes crystal clear that something needs to change.

Everyone deserves to be embodied and inhabit more of themselves.

Give yourself permission to feel whatever it is you need to feel.

Claim what you desire. Chase your wildest dreams. And above all, love yourself fully and completely.

Open your heart, drop into your body, and dive in.

Here are some steps you can take when you feel disconnected and need to get back to the flow.

- Take a Moment to Declutter Your Mind and Focus on the Present Moment
- Ask Yourself Where You Are Feeling Tension in Your Body
- Breathe Into Your Heart Space and Ask What it Wants You to Acknowledge
- Allow Feelings to Surface and Simply Hold & Accept Them Without Judgement
- Reconnect to Your Physical Body! Dance*, Practice Yoga, Walk, Massage...Whatever it Takes
- Reset Personal Boundaries with Those Around You
- Express Yourself Freely and Without Reservation

• Stay True to Yourself and Honor Your Own Needs

Would you like to explore some simple practices to help you be embodied? Here are a few of my simple go-to practices.

SHAKE IT OUT

When you are feeling anxious, this embodiment practice is for you. Stand up nice and tall. We're going to move the energy from our heads into our bodies. Imagine all the energy you're holding in and around your head right now—perhaps swirling thoughts or some fear about what I'm going to ask you to do next. Simply feel the bigness of it. Now we're going to take the energy and compress it down, move it down our bodies, and as we move it down our bodies, I invite you to start shaking and breathing like this—ha, ha, ha—and let it out. Bringing the energy down to your heart and stomach and into your hips, still with that shaking motion, and sound out any emotion and feeling noises you need to make…whatever it is, sound it out. AHHHHHHHHH. Bring all that energy down through your thighs, through your knees, let your bounce be a little heavier and slower, bring it down into your feet, feeling your feet on the ground right, wiggle your toes, bring all energy to your feet, and when you are complete, you can stop shaking. Place your hands on your stomach and inhale and exhale. Find stillness and feel grounded to your whole root. Doing this in moments of stress will help you learn to listen to your emotional and physical body and respond with what it needs.

DROPPING IN

Let's take a moment to check in to demonstrate this innate wisdom that lies within all of us. Find a quiet space to close your eyes and focus on your breath. Sitting with your eyes closed, turn your awareness to your hands and place them over your heart.

If I breathe into my heart, what does it want me to acknowledge?

After a while, start shifting your awareness to the rest of your body. As yourself, where is there tension in your body?

What can you feel in your stomach? How do your shoulders feel? How about your hips and pelvis, where we tend to store grief, frustration, and fear?

Notice where there are sensations in your body and say to yourself, "I am safe within my own body." Notice how these sensations start to shift. Be gentle with yourself and allow yourself to feel any emotions that begin to surface. Honor your own boundaries and stop if it becomes too overwhelming. But if you feel safe, just go with it and be in this state for as long as you need.

HEALING HANDS

Next time you're having a fight-or-flight response to something and are feeling panicked, stressed, or stuck, check in with your body to discover where you are feeling the stress. Simply pause and ask yourself... Where is there tension in my body? Place your hand on the area that has experienced a shift or change and breathe deeply. If it's an overall feeling, you can simply place your hands on your heart. Doing this allows the body to process the somatic experience and creates a passageway to release the tension. Notice if something comes up, an image, sensation, awareness, or understanding that offers clarity to the situation. If nothing comes up, that's okay. Simply slowing down, pacing your breath, and raising awareness is progress and helpful.

I have shared these few simple practices that you can use to reset when you feel disconnected and need to get back to the flow.

As you go about your day, I encourage you to tune in to your body whenever you need a reset.

When you know you're ENOUGH!
When you stop focusing on
all things that you're not.
When you stop fussing
over perceived flaws.
When you remove all imposed
and unbelievable
expectations on yourself.
When you start celebrating
yourself more.
When you focus on
all that you are.
When you start believing
that your perceived flaws
are just that, perception.

-Malebo Sephodi

THE TRUTH ABOUT IMPOSTOR SYNDROME

Have you ever experienced a wave of self-doubt that seemed to come out of nowhere? Has your fear stopped you from moving forward?

Have you ever felt like a fraud in your own life?

Let's be honest: who has not been kept awake at night ruminating over thoughts like...

Who am I to think that I can do this?

What will people think?

What if I fail?

I can't, I can't, I can't!

If these resonate with you, you may be suffering from what has been called Impostor Syndrome, and when it hits, it can be debilitating!

It's not really a syndrome though, is it? Nobody has a disease or illness relating to this experience. It's a pattern of thinking that makes us doubt our accomplishments and feel an overwhelming fear of being exposed as a fraud. It surfaces as that nagging feeling that you're not good enough, that you don't belong, that you don't deserve to succeed, that you have nothing of value to share. I'm here to tell you that those feelings are indeed "all in your head" and once again, based on fear.

Did you know that it's very common for high-achieving women to experience these types of feelings and to spend time explaining away their successes as not being theirs to own?

I believe in being completely transparent, so the truth is that I have spent a better part of my life being stuck in limiting belief patterns of thinking that I was unworthy. It did not matter that I was a successful entrepreneur who founded businesses and built a name for myself as an effective leader and corporate executive. At a soul level, I felt like a fraud. I spent years waiting for the ball to drop and for someone to accuse me of not earning any of it. Subconscious stories in my head made it much more comfortable for me to focus my energy on casting light on everyone else's achievements rather than my own contributions. I now understand that my hesitation was based on fear of how I would be received when I put myself out there.

When we suffer the pains of self-doubt, we often feel as though we're the only ones who have ever felt that way. That is simply not true. Even the most successful, powerful, and accomplished women (and men) have felt unsure of themselves at some point in their lives.

Some very high-profile women have shared truths about their own insecurities include:

Tina Fey: "The beauty of the impostor syndrome is you vacillate between extreme egomania and a complete feeling of: 'I'm a fraud! Oh God, they're onto me! I'm a fraud!'"

Maya Angelou: The prizewinning author once said, after publishing her eleventh book, that every time she wrote another one, she'd think to herself: "Uh-oh, they're going to find out now. I've run a game on everybody."

Michelle Obama: The former First Lady has spoken and written about how, as a young woman, she used to lie awake at night asking herself: Am I too loud? Too much? Dreaming too big? "Eventually, I just got tired of always worrying what everyone else thought of me," she said. "So, I decided not to listen."

Learning to break down the blocks and shift my mindset changed my life and led me to coaching other women going through similar transitions in life.

You are not alone—and yes, you can do this! You can rewrite the script in your head. Take a new step forward and don't fall victim to that negative self-talk. There are practical ways to overcome these insecurities, and they begin by recognizing your true value. Our thoughts and words and the language we use have real manifesting power. I encourage you to start mindfully shifting what you think and speak with the intention of boosting your own self-confidence. Here are five activities to change the way you think about yourself.

1. Make a list of your qualifications. List out at least 10 things that show you are just as qualified as anyone else for the role you are playing. Then ask yourself what evidence exists that you are any less qualified than anybody else to do this work. Is there anything that makes you more qualified?

2. Say your name out loud. Research has found that the simple act of taking a positive affirmation (such as "I'm awesome") and adding your name to it ("Jenn is awesome") can have a powerful effect on how you perceive yourself.

3. Stop comparing yourself to everyone else. You are your own unique flavor and flair.

4. Own your accomplishments. Women tend to explain their successes away by ascribing them to things like "luck," "hard work," or "help from others" rather than the innate ability or intelligence that men often cite. Try to own the role you played in your success by forbidding yourself from falling back on excuses. Practice saying these words out loud: "I'm proud of what I've accomplished."

5. Visualize your success. Visualize precisely how you'll navigate a challenging situation —successfully —before it happens. Before approaching a potential roadblock in your work, conduct a mental rehearsal of self-talk to stay under control and in the "right" mindset for the situation. Your confidence doesn't have to come only from experience—otherwise we would never try new things.

If you've talked to yourself in the mirror and made lists of your accomplishments, and you still feel that impostor feeling creeping in, try the following:

Talk to a colleague or friend. Has she felt like an impostor, too? Knowing this is a thing that others feel will help make it just that: a thing, but not your thing. If that doubting voice begins to creep into your head, repeat, "It's not me, it's the impostor syndrome talking."

Decide to be confident. Literally make the choice to be confident. Raise your hand. Volunteer your expertise. When you start spiraling into self-doubt, force yourself to write down three things you've done well.

Remind yourself you're good at what you do. Keep a folder of your own self praises to remind you of your value when you need a quick confidence boost.

Change your thoughts, and the brain will follow. You got this!

You are the creator of
your own reality.

-Esther Hickes

POSITIVE AFFIRMATIONS
AND REFLECTIONS

As women, we often find ourselves under pressure, feeling like we need to be perfect. Even for the most consciously evolved spiritual guides and healers, it's too easy to slip into critical self-talk that throws us way off balance. We have enough people criticizing us and looking to tear us down, and we do not need to jump on that bandwagon of negative energy.

I am not saying that we should push down the darkness or shadowy parts of us. As I've discussed, it is so important to honor all our parts. I also believe we need to feel all the feelings, the full range of them, and learn to recognize them in our bodies so we can receive and, in turn, process them.

What I am saying is that our thoughts and words hold so much power, and when we need to make a mindset shift, practicing positive affirmations or mantras can be very effective in taking us from a low vibration or frequency to a higher one.

I have found that implementing a positive affirmation practice is the best way to counteract the negative energy when it rears its ugly head and can effectively bring me back to a more positive place—which is where I want to be!

Positive affirmations are a way of using keywords and/or phrases to shift your thought patterns to bring energy, love, and compassion to yourself. By using positive affirmations, you can begin to write yourself a new story and drown out the inner critic with words of self-love and confidence.

Simply saying your positive affirmations aloud every day has been proven to boost your mental health, but you can also write them down or use them in a meditation practice as a mantra.

Using positive affirmations as a daily practice is essential, as the whole point is to manifest our beliefs into our reality! By repeating powerful punchy affirmations, you can kickstart your day in the best way and remind yourself that you are worthy, loved, and full of light!

Here are some of my favorite affirmations for you to practice using for yourself (also available in my Embody Your Essence Affirmation card deck):

- I am worthy
- I am deserving
- I am resilient
- I am love
- I am light
- I am healing
- I am fulfilled
- I am curious
- I am creative
- I am connected
- I am kind
- I choose me
- I love myself and others unconditionally
- I am grateful

- I am my own best advocate

- I am more than enough

- My intuition is strong and serves me well

- I trust myself

- I belong

- My feelings matter

- I am a life-long learner

- I am a spiritual seeker

- I nourish my mind and my body

- My body is a vessel of love and light

- I look and feel radiant every day

- I do not allow my past to keep me stuck

- I choose to exude confidence

- I hold all the validation I need for myself

- I do not need to impress anyone but me

- I am a vibrant being

- I am full of vitality and a passion for life

- I am a magnet for abundance

- I vibrate on a high frequency

- I make time for me every day

- I do the best I can in every given moment

- I choose my words wisely

- Nobody is judging me

- I create my own reality

- I am exactly where I need to be

- Everything is easy

- I am living in flow

- I listen to the wisdom of my body

- Good things belong to me

- It's never too late to lighten up

- I glow like a goddess

I encourage you to surround yourself in the light of self-love and flex your positive affirmations muscle on a regular basis until it becomes a second nature practice when you need a pick-me-up.

Use the following self-discovery exercises to help you ponder who you are and what is most important to you.

Self-Discovery Reflections

List my positive attributes as I AM statements. For example, I AM healthy, I AM smart, I AM resilient, I AM funny, etc.

_____

_____

_____

_____

_____

_____

_____

_____

_____

_____

_____

_____

_____

List my personal attributes or situations that I would like to improve. Please list these as "I welcome" improvements in my _____. For example, "I welcome improvements in my ability to let go of my limiting beliefs about being undeserving."

_____

_____

_____

_____

_____

_____

_____

_____

_____

_____

_____

_____

_____

_____

What has held me back from experiencing happiness and success in life? List these thoughts, feelings, emotions, limiting beliefs, resentment, etc.

_____

_____

_____

_____

_____

_____

_____

_____

_____

_____

_____

_____

_____

_____

_____

_____

Reviewing the above statements, what can I change? What actions can I take to naturally have new and rewarding experiences?

_____

_____

_____

_____

_____

_____

_____

_____

_____

_____

_____

_____

_____

_____

Which resentments or regrets am I willing to let go of? Please list these as "I am now at peace with my past and I willingly release my attachment to _____."

_____

_____

_____

_____

_____

_____

_____

_____

_____

_____

_____

_____

_____

_____

Who am I ready to forgive? Please list as "I am ready to forgive _____ for

_____."

_____

_____

_____

_____

_____

_____

_____

_____

_____

_____

_____

_____

_____

_____

_____

What habits am I ready to eliminate? Please list these as "Because I am free, I AM now able to let go of _____."

_____

_____

_____

_____

_____

_____

_____

_____

_____

_____

_____

_____

_____

What new rich and rewarding experiences, beliefs, and life-style conditions do I want to have today? Please write as "I AM now living the life I have always dreamed of. I AM now... [describe]"

_____

_____

_____

_____

_____

_____

_____

_____

_____

_____

_____

_____

_____

_____

_____

_____

You only lose
what you cling to.

~Buddha

APPRECIATE THE IMPERMANENCE

All that exists is impermanent. Nothing lasts forever.

The one true constant is that it is inevitable that circumstances, situations, relationships, emotions, and experiences will not remain the same forever.

Everything has an expiration date. Think about it. Nothing lasts forever.

Situations and circumstances change.

Thoughts and perspectives change.

Feelings change.

People change.

We cannot stop it.

Our greatest suffering seems to come when we resist changing whatever it is that is keeping us stuck.

What if we learned to accept the concept of impermanence and the fact that change is the one constant in life?

What if we stop resisting and learn to flow with more ease?

The Buddha teaches us about impermanence (Anitya)—the fact that everything changes and nothing is permanent. Our thoughts, emotions, circumstances, relationships, surroundings, and physical bodies are changing shape continuously... whether we like it or not.

Most of us are craving more peace and calm in our everyday lives, and while we cannot control the external factors unfolding around us, we can learn to manage what goes on internally. How we think, feel, and respond to the changes makes all the difference in how we experience things.

We've all heard it said that "happiness is an inside job." When I reflect on this simple truth, I am reminded to return to a place of gratitude for each moment. However, being and staying mindful takes practice, and some days go better than others.

Appreciate the moment for what it is—don't cling to it. This makes so much sense, but it's not so easy for most of us humans to put into practice.

Do you ever contemplate what the future holds and how you will feel once it gets here?

One thing is certain. The world will never look or feel the same as it does right now. The sun will rise and set again and again, but each of us, as we are today, will continue to change and evolve and show up differently.

If you truly want to be
respected by people you love,
you must prove to them
that you can survive
without them.

-Michael Bassey Johnson

ATTACHMENT VS. COMPASSIONATE DETACHMENT

According to Buddhist teachings, attachment is the root of most suffering, which explains why this concept of impermanence is so difficult for us to grasp.

We attach ourselves to things, to events, to people, to places, and to ideas. We attach because we don't understand the fundamental quality of the natural flow of life—the ebb and flow that will occur whether we like it or not.

I am coming to understand the meaning of compassionate detachment and that letting go doesn't mean we abandon a person, a dream, or an outcome.

Compassionate detachment is considered one of the most loving responses we can offer to those who we care about most. Relationships can drain us because of our mindset. We exhaust ourselves trying to fix or control another's behavior and emotional state.

Other people enhance and complement our lives, but they do not complete them. Our identity, self-worth, and value as a person has literally nothing to do with and is not dependent on another person or their actions. We are here to travel together and share experiences, but ultimately, we are here to walk our own divine path.

What if we can learn to release the entanglement? To free ourselves from pain and suffering?

We are in fact free to move toward paths that work best for our highest good. We can and should allow individuals to unfold exactly the way they are, without conditions of control or judgment.

It's a graceful surrender. When we enter a state of allowance, we liberate ourselves because we are surrendering judgment which can be so restricting and unsupportive of our well-being.

Detachment is a rare form of unconditional love. It means letting our loved ones travel in their own lane. It doesn't mean we don't care; it demonstrates that we care so much that we find the courage to allow them to travel their own path, rather than ours. I think compassionate detachment is one of the most loving responses we can offer to those who we care about most.

We do not define who we are by our success or failure in the attainment of goals or by the state of our relationships. I am learning, evolving, and warming up to this idea that everything will continue to shift, whether I cling onto it or not. So now, when I start to feel myself gripping on, I stop and simply notice what is.

Flying starts from the ground.
The more grounded you are,
the higher you fly.

-J.R. Rim

ROOTING DOWN IN TIMES OF TRANSITION

We understand this concept of impermanence and that life is ever-changing, and that detachment can help release suffering. But what do you do when change hits you out of the blue and you feel knocked off balance?

Rather than pushing back against the change, I do my best to keep an open heart full of gratitude for the colors of life and create some quiet, reflective space to breathe and examine what is happening around me. Taking a pause allows me to hit the reset button, reflect on rooting down, and redirect my energy toward new experiences.

Let's look at the change of seasons as an example. September can bring about a great deal of transition for some as we wave goodbye to the dreamy days of summer (at least, here in New England) and the fleeting time we get to spend outdoors. I feel most alive with my Jeep top open, my feet buried in the sand, sunsets, salty beach hair... summer is the season that brings me the most joy.

Then WHAM! We're hit with the back-to-school bustle, heightened work hustle, shorter days, and cooler temperatures, and a lot of us start to feel a bit more locked in! This type of transition can creep in and manifest itself in the physical body in the form of anxiety—a feeling of heaviness or nausea located in your core or lower abdomen. This can also present itself as lower back pain.

Life can feel stressful when things start to shift, and we begin to question our ability to "control" the unfolding of our own lives. The good news is that, when we can learn to root down into our bodies and notice these feelings of tension or nervousness, we become more empowered to create a better sense of peace within ourselves. When we find our own natural sense of balance, we learn to respond differently to the ever-changing dynamics that may feel as if they are swirling around us.

I work with clients to recognize, acknowledge, and accept these nervous and agitated feelings, rather than resist or ignore them, so they can begin to lovingly unravel them one at a time. This idea of learning to root down into our bodies, just like a big oak tree held up by the Earth, is a very powerful way to clear the dis-ease or whatever is "stuck there" in the energetic body that needs releasing. When we nourish and balance our body, we can stand taller amidst the change and restore ourselves with a more tranquil energy and mindset.

When you feel the overwhelm or agitation start to creep in, I recommend implementing some simple grounding practices to help restore your strength and clear negative energy from your body and mind. For me, that would be a quiet meditation, vibrational sound healing, a wild and free embodiment dance, or a gentle yoga practice. But in that very moment when anxiety hits you, I'm offering a quick two-minute practice so you can try to gain some more immediate relief.

Why? Because when we connect to the earth, we connect to something much larger than ourselves. We create a home base for our physical bodies and tap directly into our Root

Chakra. The root chakra is the seat of our core needs for life—survival, security, family, memories, traditions, taking care of ourselves, and taking care of others. It is located at the base of the spine (your tailbone) and is associated with the color red.

Simply close your eyes and focus on the Root Chakra at the base of your spine, imagining a bright ruby red wheel of light and energy spinning in a clockwise direction over the base of your spine. Reach down toward that light with your internal awareness and channel your breath into the space it occupies. Tap into your core, your center, the place where you hold all of your personal power, and drop from your head into your body. Root your feet into the Earth and let out any sounds that need to be released.

Maybe you roar like a lion or scream like a baby. Or maybe you just let out one big heavy sigh of relief. Whatever sound comes up for you, really feel it in your belly and then let it go! Release it and create space for love and light and grace. Feel rooted and calm.

When you feel stress or tightness in your body during this seasonal transition, don't allow it to paralyze you. Take a moment to tap into a full body awareness of what is happening for you and implement whatever grounding practices work best for you.

Doing this will help you replace fear and apprehension with a calm heart, a peaceful mind, and a relaxed body. As you learn to root down in times of transition, you'll empower yourself to manage unsettling experiences and challenges as they present themselves.

Daring to set boundaries
is about having the
courage to love ourselves,
even when we risk
disappointing others.

-Brené Brown

BOUNDARIES, IF YOU DARE

Many people know what the word boundary means but have no idea how to set and maintain boundaries in the practice of everyday life. You might think of boundaries as something like a property line or a "brick wall" used to keep people out. But boundaries are not rigid lines drawn in the sand that are clear for all to see.

Boundaries are simply a way to take better care of ourselves. When you understand how to set and maintain healthy boundaries, you can avoid the feelings of resentment, disappointment, and anger that build up when limits have been pushed.

Boundaries can take many forms. They can range from being rigid and strict to appearing almost nonexistent.

A person with healthy boundaries understands that making their expectations clear helps in two ways: it establishes what behavior you will accept from other people, and it establishes what behavior other people can expect from you.

If you have healthy boundaries, you might:

- share personal information appropriately (not too much or too little)
- understand your personal needs and clearly communicate them
- value your own opinions
- accept when others tell you "no" without negativity

Many of us have a mix of boundaries depending on the situation. For example, you might have more strict boundaries at work and more loose ones at home or with family and friends.

I continually vow to set and maintain healthier boundaries and admit that this still a work in progress. As mentioned, I'm a nurturer with a built-in tendency to want to rescue people. While this is a wonderful gift to others, I've learned that too much of a good thing can leave me feeling depleted and resentful. When this happens, I find myself vibrating on a much lower frequency than where I want to be, so I give myself a swift kick in the pants to mindfully taking actions for my highest good.

In my work with women, I teach them that creating boundaries is very empowering and is, in fact, essential for our overall well-being. When we set and manage expectations and limits for ourselves, we protect our own self-esteem, maintain self-respect, and learn to separate our thoughts/feelings from others. Nobody wants their boundaries violated by others. Yet we've all experienced times when we've allowed lines to be crossed. We need to learn to differentiate between where our own values start and stop and where another's begin.

It can be tricky to maintain boundaries, especially with those closest to us. Even though we're all separate beings, we can get lost in our connectedness with one another and the lines get blurry. Most struggle to maintain healthy boundaries out of fear of the response we'll get from someone we care about, or out of guilt for not doing enough for that person.

Even though it can go against our nature to put our own needs first, I encourage you to give yourself permission to put some self-preservation guidelines in place.

This will look different for each of us, but main principles are to:

- Assess your personal boundaries first—what do you need?
- Communicate clearly and kindly, without raising your voice, and focus on what you want, not what you don't want/need.
- Safeguard your time and space to preserve your energy.
- Avoid feeling guilt or shame for setting boundaries for yourself.

Remember, a healthy relationship allows you the space to be yourself and to maintain your personal integrity. Most people will respect your boundaries when you explain what they are and will expect you to do the same for them. I know from experience that when I consciously honor my boundaries, I live a more balanced life and enjoy more productive and loving relationships—and you can too.

When you see yourself
clearly with eyes full of love
and acceptance,
you hold space for others
to meet you at your highest self.

-Karly Ryan

HOLDING SPACE

As the founder of a wellness center, I make the commitment to hold space for growth and healing every day. But what does it really mean to hold space?

To me, it means being fully present—physically, mentally, and emotionally—for another person or group of people. It means listening without wanting anything back from a place of empathy and compassion. Holding space means accepting someone's truth, no matter who they are or what they believe, and to simply allow and accept what is.

My center was mindfully designed to be a safe container where members and guests come to have meaningful experiences. We have created a nourishing environment where people can lean into us for support without fear of judgment. We foster an inclusive community where everyone is welcome to approach their healing journey in their own time and in their own way. We like to believe we are doing our part to raise the collective vibration of the world, and we encourage all members of our community to do the same.

When we love and accept one another unconditionally, we allow everyone to simply be and to feel what they need to feel without worrying about how they are being perceived. I realize that the art of holding space is not something that is taught to us, and it is not easy to do it without feeling the urge to step in and "fix things." But I invite you to think of a time when you felt vulnerable.

What would have helped you most in that moment?

Did you need someone to step in, give you advice, or solve your problem?

Or would it have been enough to simply have someone to be there for you, holding the space for you to find your own way?

Sitting with someone in loving support and free from judgment can help them feel seen, understood, and less alone.

It is such a gift when we hold space for another person—but don't forget the importance of learning to hold space for yourself and recognizing when you need to ask for support from others. Holding space does not mean allowing people to walk all over you. Nobody likes to feel taken for granted when their intention was to help someone in need. Empaths and healers run the risk of giving out too much of their energy and then feeling drained. That's why it's important for all of us to remember to set and maintain healthy boundaries.

We keep hearing about the importance of holding space for others, but do we also remember to hold space for ourselves when we need it? If we don't care for ourselves and tend to our own needs first, we run the risk of burning out and becoming bitter or resentful.

Treat yourself with the same love, compassion, and empathy that you would treat a client, a friend, or a loved one. It can be challenging to observe your own thoughts and feelings and to release attachment from outcomes. I know from personal experience how unnatural it feels for me to sit with something instead of taking corrective action. This is where daily mindfulness practices can help us to tune in and practice surrendering and loosening the controls so we can hold space for ourselves and for one another with the purest of intentions and for the highest good of all.

Here are some ways you can hold space for yourself:

1. Practice mindfulness, which simply means staying in the present moment. Rather than trying to stop the racing thoughts from coming, simply notice them and let them pass by without judgment.

2. Learn when to walk away from draining people and situations. You can't serve other people well when your energy is depleted.

3. When emotions surface, allow your tears to flow when they need to flow. It's a great way to release stuck energy from your body.

4. Allow others to hold space for you when you need it. We all need community and opportunities to show up for one another.

5. Find sources of inspiration. There are many writers, artists, and musicians who can inspire you to replenish your soul and hold space for yourself.

When gratitude becomes
an essential foundation
in our lives,
miracles start to
appear everywhere.

-Emmanuel Dagher

PRACTICE GRATITUDE

We have already learned the importance of being present and mindful and having a positive attitude. It's been proven that focusing on positive thoughts and behaviors helps improve our overall health and well-being.

The emotions that keep us vibrating on a higher frequency include optimism, hope, and, you guessed it, gratitude!

Gratitude is the expression of appreciation for what one has. It is spontaneously generated from within. It is an affirmation of goodness and warmth.

Simply put, practicing gratitude is good for you. There's so much to be gained from being genuinely grateful. Research has linked gratitude with a wide range of benefits, including strengthening the immune system and improving sleep patterns, feeling optimistic and experiencing more joy and pleasure, being more resilient, and feeling less lonely and isolated. It even helps to overcome depression.

Gratitude Improves Relationships

Can you recall a time when you had a knee-jerk reaction to refuse a gift or gesture from someone? Maybe your impulse was that it was not deserved or simply "too much." What would happen if you didn't get involved in that narrative, and just allowed yourself to accept the gift or the kindness and allow yourself to receive it and to feel... grateful? There's scientific evidence that feeling and expressing gratitude in relationships reinforces and strengthens them.

Gratitude is Good for the Collective

It's easy to feel gratitude for help offered when we're in need—a stranger who smiles at you on the street, or the friend who brings you soup when you're sick. We need to stop and consider what it is that motivates us to help one another and how we are all so interconnected. A tiny act of kindness ripples outward into something much bigger than any one of us alone—and spreading that kind of kindness makes a lasting impact.

A Simple Mindful Gratitude Exercise

Building your capacity for gratitude isn't difficult. It just takes practice.

The more you can bring your attention to that which you feel grateful for, the more you'll attract into your life to be grateful for.

Start by observing and notice the thank you(s) you say. How are you feeling when you express thanks in small transactions? Stressed, uptight, a little absent-minded? Do a quick scan of your body—are you already physically moving on to your next interaction?

When your instinct to say "thanks" pops up, stop in the present moment. Name exactly what is that you feel grateful for, even beyond the gesture that's been extended. Then say thank you more mindfully.

Keep a Gratitude Journal

Spend 15 minutes per day, at least once per day, for at least two weeks, on a gratitude journal practice. Studies suggest that writing in a gratitude journal three times per week might have a greater impact on our overall happiness than journaling every day.

There's no right or wrong way to keep a gratitude journal, but here are some general guidelines as you get started.

Write down up to five things for which you feel grateful.

The physical record is important—don't just do this exercise in your head. The things you list can be relatively small in importance like, "I am grateful for my warm cup of coffee."

The gift in this practice is to take a mindful pause to remember a good event, experience, person, or thing in your life—then enjoy the good emotions that come with it.

As you write, here are some mindful writing tips:

1. Be as specific as possible —Specificity is key to fostering gratitude. "I'm grateful that my colleague helped me out today because I was able to meet my deadline" will be more effective than "I'm grateful for my coworker."

2. Go for depth over breadth. Elaborating in detail about a particular person or thing for which you're grateful carries more benefits than a superficial list of many things.

3. Get personal. Focusing on the people, including yourself, and experiences that you are grateful for has more of an impact than focusing on things for which you are grateful.

4. See good things as "gifts." Thinking of the good things in your life as gifts helps us savor the moments so we do not take them for granted.

5. Delight in surprises. Try to record events that were unexpected or surprising, as these tend to elicit stronger levels of gratitude.

6. Journal regularly. Whether you write your Gratitudes every other day or once a week, commit to a regular time to journal, then honor that commitment.

*Everything in
life is a vibration.*

-Albert Einstein

RAISE YOUR VIBRATION

I am an Energy Junkie, and the more I explore it, the more addicted I become to working with energy in all aspects of my life.

Everything in the universe is energy—every rock, tree, chair, animal, and living being. People are energy, and our thoughts and emotions hold the positive or negative frequency that make up who we are as unique individuals.

When we refer to a person's energy, we're simply referring to YOU, your Higher Soul, Self, or Source. When you're aligned with your heartfelt desires and your intuitive knowing, you are aligned to your Higher Self—and you're vibrating at higher frequency.

When you're in tune with you, you raise your vibrational frequency and attract even more positive energy, people, and situations around you.

Our energetic vibration attracts similar frequencies, so when we operate on a higher frequency, we attract other people vibing higher. The Law of Attraction is a philosophy that claims one's thoughts determines their reality. This practice includes mindful strategies such as positive self-talk, and visualization to create a world we want to live in. I believe in the power of manifestation. It works!

Developing an energetic intuition and awareness will significantly improve your life. You will feel more grounded and open to possibilities. You will communicate with more clarity and power. You will send a higher vibration out into the world around you and begin to see everything shift. You will experience life with more ease and abundance.

It is challenging to stay in that high-vibe state, in alignment and connected to Source every day. That's why I'm doing this work. I want to help women facing life's transitions to learn how to work with energy, how to stay connected and attract higher frequencies, and how to manifest an abundant life.

Remember, your vibration is simply the energy that you're sending out, which is also what you're attracting to you. Energy attracts like energy.

Your feelings and emotions impact your vibration. When you notice yourself feeling negatively about anything or anyone, become consciously aware and try to shift that energy back into alignment. To shift your energy, you can stop yourself in that moment and just breathe deeply, meditate, go outside and take a walk, or put on your favorite song and dance it out.

The more aligned you are with your Higher Self and Source, to what makes your soul feel full, the happier and healthier you will be, and life will begin to flow effortlessly through you. You get to choose.

It is your divine right
and your spiritual duty
to protect your energy field
from unwanted influences.

-Anthon St. Maarten

PROTECT YOUR ENERGY

I teach my students about the importance of learning how to develop self-defense strategies for protecting their energy.

When you can more mindfully manage your energy by setting healthy boundaries, you will intentionally cultivate more joy in your life. Recognize when something doesn't feel good to you. Learn to walk away and to make whatever change is necessary to preserve your own mental wellness.

As mentioned earlier, we all learned in middle school science class that everything is made up of energy. What they don't teach in schools, however, is that the way in which we show up and interact with one another's energy fields as human beings can have a major impact on how we feel and experience the world.

Whether you consider yourself an empath or not, learning how to tune in and manage your own energy and respond to the energy of others is a necessary Superpower. Maintaining balance in our own lives and in our relationships is an ongoing practice of learning how to protect yourself and your energy in all kinds of situations. There are basic self-defense techniques a person can learn and to help stay balanced and well. It begins with an awareness of your own space and mindset and a conscious decision to keep your thoughts and emotions positive! It's also about shielding yourself from negative energy, which can include people and circumstances. And finally, it's important to maintain an adequate amount of mental, physical, and spiritual energy of your own so you avoid energy depletion or burnout, which occur when too much of our energy is going outward to others.

Some simple self-defense strategies include:

Be Aware of the Energy Around You. Sometimes, energy protection is about noticing how others' energies might trigger something in you. If you find yourself feeling ignited by someone else's vibe in a negative way (like anger, stress, etc.), simply use whatever is coming up for you to reflect on where that matching energy lives within you. Life is a mirror, and how others affect you can help bring awareness to an experience and what it is telling you. When you do this, you allow space for that energy to move and heal within yourself.

Set and Maintain Healthy Boundaries. One of the best ways to protect your energy is to set and maintain boundaries that serve you best. This practice can look different for everyone, depending on what boundaries they need around other people. For some of us, particularly us empaths, sticking to our boundaries can be challenging (especially if you are one of those who people are drawn to). It's not easy to draw an energetic line in the sand, and you may lose people along the way, but your own self-preservation is of the utmost importance, because empathy without boundaries is self-destruction.

Allow Yourself Space to Recharge. Give yourself the time and space to recharge so you don't run your own battery down to nothing. Energy burnout is real! I have been there. Do what you can to preserve your own energy and fuel up your reserve, whether that means spending more time alone or only with others who can support and replenish your energy levels (not drain them).

Use Visualization. When you feel an energy vampire nearby, stop to pause, close your eyes, and visualize yourself surrounded in a white light or bubble that cannot be penetrated by outside forces. This exercise raises your vibration, shields you from negativity, and helps to neutralize the negative vibrations that are trying to make their way into your aura. The white light visualization can also be used to reset after encountering others' energies. You can also take a shower and visualize the water washing away all the energy that you have collected throughout the day, sending it down the drain forever.

Get Grounded. In today's culture, many of us spend most of our days with our nervous system in a sympathetic state, or fight-or-flight mode, which impacts our energy and how we are affected by others' energies. The best way to stabilize your nervous system and protect your own energy field is to get grounded. You can do that by meditating, conscious breath work, taking a walk, gardening, or whatever mindful act works best for you.

Attitude of Gratitude. When you encounter someone who has an aura of uncomfortable energy, a gratitude practice can help diffuse the situation. Gratitude is a high vibrational, powerful emotion that will lead to an immediate energy shift through thoughts and feelings of kindness, love, and appreciation.

Sage, Crystals, and Sprays... Oh My! I have a toolbox of essential oil sprays for clearing spaces. I burn sage to clear the lower chakras and palo santo for the upper chakras. Crystals are a must and can be carried or placed in your physical surroundings to manage the vibes, because they hold high vibrational energy and can both attract and protect against certain energies. Everyone has their favorite gems made by Mother Earth, but I tend to rely on hematite, black tourmaline, selenite, and tiger' eye in my spaces. And you'll always find salt lamps and a fresh bowl of pink himalayan sea salt in my healing rooms.

For me, the most important self-defense strategy is that of pure intention. I hold in my mind and heart the belief that my thoughts and actions are the highest and best for myself and others and that good intentions always beat out the bad. We all have the choice to put more good out into the world, to consciously practice positive energy, implement energy protection techniques, and to dispel uncomfortable energies by protecting our own boundaries.

Do not go with the flow.

Be the flow.

-Elif Shafak

FIND YOUR FLOW

You know that feeling when you are totally in sync with the world around you? You trust that the Universe has your back and everything is happening in divine order.

You have an abundance of energy and feel inspired to spread positivity everywhere you go. You believe with your whole heart that everything you want and need is already flowing to you and that life is amazing!

Perhaps it's been a while since you've felt this way. But it is that very state of flow that I aspiring to. A flow state, also known as being in the zone, is when a person is performing an activity in which they are fully immersed with energized focus, full involvement, and pure enjoyment. To be in the flow means that you are consciously being in harmony with whatever it is you are doing in that moment. Sounds wonderful, doesn't it? But that begs the question... how do we fall out of the flow?

The culprit is resistance. What we resist, persists. We are all made up of energy and energy is in constant motion... so it makes perfect sense that when we resist something, things will stop flowing naturally. When you start to feel out of the flow, simply ask yourself if you're forcing something that doesn't align with your true intentions. Determine what is blocking you from moving forward. Most of our blockages come from lingering limiting beliefs that were shaped in our formative years and reside in our subconscious mind for years to come until we uncover and unblock them.

The good news is that each new moment provides us the opportunity to shift our mindset and change course. By mindfully bringing awareness to our thoughts and feelings we can significantly modify our behaviors. This shift helps us make the transition to a place of allowing—a state of mind where we trust things to unfold as they are meant to unfold—and find our way back into balance and harmony. Once you shift your mindset and align with these energy patterns, it can still be challenging to stay in the flow, because life happens and we get knocked off balance from time to time. But don't give up.

Take a quiet moment to tap into your intuition and listen to your inner guidance. Notice any physical signs from your body that may be showing signs of distress, then breathe slowly and mindfully into those areas. Pay attention to your emotions and then consciously choose to take actions that bring you back to center. Finding and staying in the flow is a continual practice. It's a state of evolution, but returning to it time and time again is worthwhile. I look forward to my practice of living in the flow and hope you enjoy the journey of your own personal growth and expansion in the days, weeks, and months to come.

The openness of our hearts
determines the quality
of our lives.

-Unknown

KEEP AN OPEN HEART

What does it mean to live with an open heart? We hear about keeping our hearts open in our yoga practices, in our guided meditations, and in the self-improvement books and blogs we read to stay in the flow. But what does it really mean to have an open heart, and more importantly, how do we keep it open, especially when life can knock us down to our knees at times?

An open heart is a state of being where we feel receptive, accepting, and forgiving. Love flows through us freely and without obstruction. When we have an open heart, we can connect with our true selves, discover our highest potential, and live in peace with the world around us. We see the good in people and focus on sparking genuine human connection.

It takes work to keep our hearts open because it means resisting the natural human tendency to shut down and build walls to protect ourselves from being hurt by others. We can physically feel it when our hearts start to close. We get a tightness in our chest and our fight-or-flight reflex kicks in. We feel paralyzed, stuck, angry, and resentful. But that is when we have a choice to make. Do we let fear take us down and imprison us? Or do we dig deeper to find the courage to open our hearts and be vulnerable?

Brené Brown says "allowing oneself to become wholehearted requires an act of courage. Yet it can lead us down the path of greater happiness and connection." It is only when we approach life from a place of openness that we can embody connectedness with all things.

The way to an open art begins when we can embrace our own vulnerability. It's very empowering when we allow ourselves a safe space to be vulnerable and to examine our own thoughts and emotions. We all want the same thing—to be loved and accepted for who we really are and for others to understand that we are doing our best. Next, it is important to release judgments and keep a forgiving heart and mind toward the person or circumstances that may have harmed or caused us suffering. We create stories and boundaries that divide us, yet there is freedom that comes in stripping those away and in letting go of unwanted emotions that weigh us down. When we find ourselves retreating into that space of fear, we can ask ourselves how important that person or relationship is to us and how we might shift our approach to deliberately live in love... and to stay open.

I encourage you to hold an open heart for yourself as well as for other people. As women, we are typically quite good at nurturing our friends and family during their times of need. But we often forget to hold that same safe and supportive space for ourselves.

As part of the experience, I encourage you to create quiet, reflective time to:

1. breathe into your painful emotions
2. listen to the messages of your heart
3. find clarity about what you want and need, and
4. craft the words to improve connections with others from a place of greater expansion and love.

When we can learn how to trust and open our hearts to ourselves and to one another in this way, we can live a more joyful and vibrant existence with enriching life experiences and connectedness.

There is a crack in everything.
That is how the light gets in.

-Unknown

NEVER TOO LATE TO LIGHTEN UP

I shared my personal stories to illustrate how every one of us has been through loss, tragedy, and pain. We all have subconscious limiting beliefs about our worthiness and our ability to be loved, and we all have the power to tap into our own minds to create positive change and elevate our lives.

My life's suffering was based on experiencing trauma, resulting in my own self-loathing, unhealthy attachments, and limiting beliefs that did not serve me. For most of my life, I was seeking validation from others versus seeking love and acceptance from within. I took myself and everyone around me way too seriously, and I know now that all my choices were driven by my limiting beliefs that I was unlovable, undeserving, and unworthy of happiness.

Even now, after years of unraveling, I continue to look deep into the shadows and do mindset work to release attachment to people and outcomes that are not mine to own.

By doing the work, I've realized that I needed to lighten up the load I was carrying and release myself from self-inflicted pain and suffering.

Maybe it was time to stop "rescuing" others? Maybe the real relationship I most needed to foster was the one with myself? To learn to see my own value, my own worth, and to believe that I was in fact deserving of love?

This is a journey so many of us find ourselves on, and it can take decades to get to the destination where things become clear to us. If only we understood these traps earlier in life so we could redirect and rewire our thought patterns and learn to start with self-love! If I could go back in a time machine and share advice with a younger me, I would say...

- Lighten up! Release your burdens and don't take yourself too seriously.
- Stop putting so much emphasis on what everyone else thinks about you, because we are not here to please others.
- Take risks. Don't be afraid to make mistakes—simply learn from them.
- Our journey is to be here in Earth School to learn how to feed our own soul... to love and accept ourselves.
- You are enough JUST AS YOU ARE. You don't have to prove yourself or earn it.
- Enjoy the ride and have more fun!

I have said it before: it is never too late to release what no longer serves you and begin again. Release. Reveal. Radiate!

I will never dim my glow simply because someone is intimidated by my radiance.

~Unknown

RECLAIM YOUR JOY

So here you are, Beautiful Soul, at the end of my story and the beginning of yours.

I hope you found inspiration in my words and found the personal courage to step up, stand out, and shine your light out into the world as only you can do. You are a rare and precious miracle... one in 400 trillion chances of being born as you. And you are here to show up and share your gifts to help connect with others who need what only you can offer them. You are more than enough!

It's time to ...

- Release what does not serve you!
- Reveal the deepest parts of you and own your story!
- Feel to heal it (moving through pain is the only way)!
- Radiate your light!

I SEE you...

- You are a precious expression of the Sacred Feminine
- You are a one-of-a-kind gem
- You are a source of light and brilliance
- Use your light to illuminate others, to lift up a world that needs your love, your positivity, and your healing energy
- It is your time to shine so bright

We are all beings of light with limitless possibilities. It is through our connection to our own light that we can see beyond the constructs of our physical surroundings. We are often taught not to believe in things we cannot see, that magic is not real, and that we only get this one lifetime to "get it right."

DO NOT LET ANYONE DIM YOUR LIGHT!

At the very core of your being, there is your deepest knowing—the "I am" statement—that reminds you of who you are and the magic that you can create.

Life has always been very unpredictable for everyone on the planet. Many of us are reawakening to a new level of consciousness and reflecting on our own truths and insights.

The good news is that we're learning to tap in and trust our inner knowing about what we've been experiencing and how we are responding to things that feel so out of our control.

What if our challenges have presented us with an opportunity to reconnect to our own inner light so we can find clarity? We have everything we need to live the life we desire. Allowing yourself to believe in your dream is the first step to manifesting it.

Make it a daily practice to pause, breathe, meditate, move your body, get out into nature, commune with others, and reclaim whatever it is you want and need to access your full potential with a brave heart and warrior-like spirit.

As each of us connects with our own inner light, we can raise the collective vibration and begin to witness magnificent and measurable shifts all around us.

Just for fun, I have included a special gift for you. I hope you will fully immerse yourself in the Glow Like a Goddess Guide in the pages that follow to help you step out into the light as only you can.

Rise, Sister, Rise, and Reclaim Your Joy!

What is a Goddess?

A woman who is in the process of
learning to know, accept and
love herself on all levels.
Mind, Body, and Spirit.
A woman who, because she focuses
on personal growth and self-awareness,
experiences a life,
increasingly filled with
peace, love, joy, passion, and fun.
A woman who understands
that she has unlimited capacity
to make her life anything she wants.
A woman who is inspired to give to
hose around her because of her sense
of gratitude and abundance.

~Unknown

GLOW LIKE A
GODDESS GUIDE

WE'VE COME A
LONG WAY, BABY

Women have been suffering oppression for far too long. Some of my readers may recall this section's headline from an old Virginia Slims cigarette commercial in the 1970s, and while I am certainly not a proponent of destroying your lungs with nicotine or foreign substances of any kind, the subliminal message of women on the road to finding their own independence always resonated with me. It is interesting to reflect on the history of feminism to understand how we got to where we are today. We may have come a long way, but we still have many miles to go!

Did you know...

- Women were considered property only 200 years ago
- It's only been 100 years since white women fought and won the right to vote (women of color had to wait until 1975 for voting rights)

- In 1960, a woman could not get access to birth control without her husband's permission
- The Equal Pay Act was first put into effect in 1963 by President John F. Kennedy, but we are still fighting that battle
- Women could not have their own credit cards until 1974
- Our right to choose what we do with our own bodies is still being debated

It's hard to believe, but women continue to receive mixed messages regarding how we are expected to behave to meet social norms. We're told what we should and should not do, how to act, and what is and is not an acceptable way for us to behave.

From a young age, women are encouraged to look like the models in the magazines, while on the other hand we are shunned for "dressing like a slut" and taunting males who cannot control their sexual urges. We're taught in schools to stand up and speak our truth, while on the other hand, we're expected to blend in and not be confrontational. We're told we can work hard to become strong, confident leaders, while on the other hand, we shouldn't be too loud, bossy, or outspoken.

It's no wonder we're confused about which energies to draw upon. We are all very grateful for the feminist movement and to those brave women who fought and secured the rights we have today. But did you ever think about the fact that, in our fight for equality, we inadvertently sent the wrong message that women needed to act more like men?

Women don't want to be more like men. We just want to be extended the same liberties and opportunities. In some ways, our battle for equality may have led us to take on more of the masculine characteristics and tendencies to prove our worthiness and to be taken more seriously when all we needed to do was relax into our sacred feminine power—to release, accept, allow, and receive—and then watch how more ease unfolds.

While it served her in the past,
she refused to keep
her magic contained,
restrained, or detained any longer.

-Rebecca Campbell

WHAT IS THE SACRED FEMININE?

When we refer to the Sacred or Divine Feminine, what do we mean? Quite simply, it is a form of energy that all human beings possess. The Sacred Feminine describes our connection to the Mother Goddess; this internal power gives us life and calls us to her. Often associated with kindness and compassion, the fire inside each one of us is much more than meets the eye!

The Sacred Feminine is the healing feminine force that connects people to nature, to one another, and to all sources of energy. It's known by many names, such as Shakti, yin, and lunar energy, and is often connected symbolically with the moon, Gaia (Mother Earth), and water.

When I teach women about the Sacred Feminine, I often refer to it as Shakti, a concept in Hindu mythology that represents divine, cosmic feminine energy. In its simplest terms, Shakti is a force so strong that it evokes liberation and freedom to the female spirit.

Shakti is said to have brought about creation, and its force can be manifested to make space for new life and change. Once that change unfolds, Shakti generates more balance and peace to the new direction unfolding.

Sacred Feminine energy is part of everyone's wholeness and, just like the Masculine, the Feminine is only half of the whole. We need both energies to be complete. Her energy lives within all beings of all gender identities and expressions. When we learn to tune into the energy of the Sacred Feminine, we bring forth qualities of nurturing, compassion, and healing.

But do not mistake any of those feminine energies as being submissive or weak in any way, shape, or form. Honoring the sacred feminine is about embodying our fullest and most empowered version of ourselves as a person who recognizes her worth, speaks her truth, owns her sexuality, and commands the respect she deserves.

When we divide all human experiences into the gender categories, we lose the opportunity to access wholeness. To find our way back to a loving, kind way of being, we need to nurture the universal values that belong to the Sacred Feminine. It's no secret that there have been imbalances between the masculine and the feminine energies for far too long.

The conversation that needs to be had is not about creating more imbalance between the genders, but about bringing both masculine and feminine energies into a more equal and harmonious state of balance. Every one of us possesses masculine and feminine energies, and they both have value. Masculine energy is more dominant, direct, and structured, and it is a "doing" energy. Feminine energy is receptive, intuitive, ever-changing, and fluid, and is seen as a "being" energy.

The gentleness of the Sacred Feminine can be an important part of everyone's wholeness if we allow it to surface. When I relax into my divine feminine and stop forcing everything, I experience more freedom and flow. It feels effortless to focus my energy on more being and less doing. I invite you to awaken your divine feminine energies to find a deeper connection to your intuition and be more in alignment with your higher self.

When we look at the current qualities dominating modern life today, we see an overemphasis on masculine qualities in that "success" is defined by achievements, competition, and pushing things forward. This may have been necessary in another time for survival, but it has led our society to a breakdown in our ecosystems, political upheaval, war, social injustices, and poor overall health. We need to learn to rely on more feminine qualities of love, acceptance, and nurturing ourselves and others with the intention of promoting growth and healing.

Each of us has an opportunity to surrender into some of those more feminine tendencies to help heal the world. The world needs more compassion, empathy, and warmth, which are the tendencies of femininity. Every person, whether male, female, or nonbinary, holds both feminine and masculine energies and qualities. While women tend to feel a deeper connection to humanity, we all have access to these healing energies. As individuals, we can consciously live more fully in our own divine feminine energy by resisting less, receiving more willingly, and learning to accept things exactly as they are in the present moment.

As a collective, we can practice more love, compassion, patience, and understanding to bring about more peace and less conflict. So where do we go from here? We cannot rely on our old way of doing things, because we were way out of balance and that just isn't working any longer. We all breathe the same air and want to live in a kinder, more loving world. It's time to do some collaborative dreaming of what we want our future to hold.

DROPPING INTO YOUR FEMININE

Do you know how to drop into your sacred feminine energy? If not, you are not alone. The truth is that women are rarely taught how to connect with their own innate power. Many women have learned to take on more masculine characteristics to get ahead in life. We're encouraged to set goals, work hard, climb the corporate ladder, put others' needs before our own, and find the perfect work/life balance.

And let's not forget to mention that we are expected to look good while doing it! We have all been stuck in that place where we feel depleted from the constant pushing, pushing, pushing. While our culture admires this type of behavior, it can be a dangerous cycle. I know when I am vibrating on this lower frequency, I feel lost and confused and sometimes even a bit resentful of my relationships. We need to surrender into our divine feminine energy so we can stop resisting and start flowing. Feminine energy is radiant, beautiful, and full of grace. It inspires creativity and expansion.

A true Goddess attracts what she wants by just "being" in her natural state of flow. When you're leading in love with the divine feminine, life feels easy and effortless. You are sensual. You feel connected with your own intuition. You trust the universe and open yourself up to receiving an abundance of blessings. You feel full and completely in alignment with your higher self. Can you remember a time when you experienced that state of freedom? It can be challenging to find and stay in this state of flow. Most of us have had our femininity shamed, so it's an instinct to replace it with a tough, thick skin. We're taught not to be too emotional or to expose our vulnerability. It is the societal conditioning to block the flow of energies that are natural to us that has thrown women off balance. This is not to say that masculine energy is bad, because it isn't. Women need to exercise their masculine energies to set and manage expectations, maintain healthy boundaries, and take necessary action from time to time. Your masculine side helps hold space for your divine feminine to show up and for you to feel safe being authentically you.

Men have also been pigeon-holed by societal pressures and expected to embody all the "doing" attributes of masculine energy. Just like women, most men have not been taught to embody their own masculine energy in a healthy, productive manner. To make matters worse, men are not allowed to express any of their feminine characteristics without being seen as weak or passive. Everything is about finding the right balance. It is our job, as the drivers of this new consciousness team, to honor both the divine feminine and the masculine to bring them back into perfect harmony.

GODDESS UP

The question I hear most often from the women I work with is "how do I relax into my divine feminine?" That's my cue to say Goddess Up, Baby! A Goddess is a woman who is in the process of rebirthing herself. It's time for a radical awakening to shed your old skin. When you Goddess Up, you learn to live authentically from your sacred feminine. You question everything you've learned about who you are and how the world works.

You reconnect with your physical body (your vessel) and learn to trust your own inner energy. You trust your own desires. You trust life. You use your masculine energy in ways that help you, not drain you. You use your feminine energy to experience pleasure, to surrender, to flow, and to attract everything you desire into your life. Women everywhere are tuning into their sacred feminine to find more harmony and flow in their lives. We are the changemakers charged with shaking things up and leading the way toward a new global consciousness. We are shaping new ways of being that have never been here before. And our time is now!

Saying the things that have been long been left unsaid. Remembering long forgotten wisdom. The fierce feminine is changing the landscape now and forever. We need to Goddess Up, reclaim our power, and rise up from the ashes like the phoenix who is here to spread goodness and return us to the light. The process of bringing forth more feminine power is not for the faint-hearted, so don't expect it to be easy. It may bring up a lot of old wounds and scars that have held you back until now. It's like birthing a child, as new life pushes its way through such a small space. It can be excruciating and exhausting, but so worth it when the miracle appears.

It's time for women around the globe to rebirth themselves. To grow, evolve, and kick and scream at the top of your lungs to be heard! No matter what shape this birthing process takes for you, you're likely to experience emotional ups and downs full of self-examination and doubt. I encourage you to just keep breathing as you kick and scream your way through it... it is your feminine energy rising within you, and it will all be worth it in the end when the new Goddess in you emerges.

Every time we are called to evolve, we are shedding parts of ourselves that no longer serve us to create space for new growth and healing. This process of rebirth will be continually rising within you. Pain and suffering in life are inevitable. Use it and transform your new-found feminine into personal power. Let it feed and inspire you and prepare you for deep expansion on every level.

GODDESS ACTIVATION PRACTICES

Activating Your Sacred Feminine Energy

It's important to gain an understanding of how you really feel about femininity and why you feel the way you do. Most women do not embody the instinctual, sensual parts of themselves. They are sleepwalking through their lives, feeling tired and overwhelmed, lacking passion and out of sync with their own creative energy. If this sounds like you, remember you're not alone.

Limiting Beliefs About Femininity are real. A big part of accessing our Feminine Power is to identify old stories and determine how they are impacting the way you're showing up in YOUR life.

Reflections

What has society or your parents taught you about femininity (good or bad)?

_____

_____

_____

_____

_____

_____

_____

_____

_____

_____

_____

_____

_____

_____

_____

_____

_____

What positive or negative beliefs have you developed surrounding femininity?

_____

_____

_____

_____

_____

_____

_____

_____

_____

_____

_____

_____

_____

_____

What habits and behaviors do you practice that may support or oppress the Sacred Feminine?

_____

_____

_____

_____

_____

_____

_____

_____

_____

_____

_____

_____

_____

_____

_____

_____

_____

_____

Positive Mantras to Activate the Feminine

You've heard of the Law of Attraction. Life is not just happening to you—it is responding to you. What we think about and speak about, we literally attract into our lives. We are that powerful when we learn to control our thoughts and choose our words more mindfully.

Limiting Belief Positive Affirmation

I say "yes" when I mean "no_____

I lack time/money/resources _____

Other women trigger me _____

I lack confidence_____

I'm not worthy_____

I dim my light for others _____

I feel isolated and alone _____

Own Who You Are!

You cannot stand in your full radiant Goddess power unless you know who you are and learn to own it—all the good and the bad, the light and the dark, the strengths and the weaknesses. When you know who you are, no one can take away your power, bring you down, or limit your potential. Perhaps your uniqueness is what makes others feel inferior or uncomfortable. So what? Own it anyway!

Write a list of six things that are all true about you-your light and your dark. Own it all, shame-free!

The Light

1. _____

2. _____

3. _____

4. _____

5. _____

6. _____

The Dark

1. _____

2. _____

3. _____

4. _____

5. _____

6. _____

What if your so-called dark side or your weakness is in fact what makes you shine the brightest when you decide to own it? Think of a time when you have been accused of being "too much," "too bossy," or "too emotional."

How did that make you feel? More importantly, how can you nurture this perceived weakness and realign your life so that your "fault" becomes your gift?

_____

_____

_____

_____

_____

_____

_____

_____

_____

_____

_____

_____

Tapping Into Your Intuition

In working through these contemplative exercises, it is common for women to default back to our masculine forms of energy and start focusing on goals and strategies for getting what we want and need. When you feel yourself falling back into those habits, I urge you to stop and pull out your divine feminine power tools. Focus on higher frequency type energies like self-acceptance, self-love, self-actualization, creativity, contribution, and communication.

Tap in your inner wisdom and your intuition to connect to the deeper truths from within. We all hold a deeper intelligence—our intuition. Intuition is not highly valued in our culture. We are taught to not trust ourselves and our inner knowing at a very young age. Most of us have been trained to trust more logical approaches of strategizing and planning. The truth is that we all have so much wisdom inside of us that we can call upon whenever we need answers. If your life isn't working the way you want it to, give some thought to how well you connect to your own inner knowing.

Listen to it. Trust it. Act on it. When you practice listening, trusting, and acting on your own intuition, you will have a divine feminine breakthrough and access that unstoppable power within you. You will gain the clarity you are seeking. You will feel empowered and become more confident in yourself and in your decisions. Your life will start to flow with ease.

Reflections

Think about a decision you need to make but have been avoiding. Maybe this decision has been spinning around in your head and, for some reason, you have been unable to move forward. Notice any tension in your body as you bring this challenge to mind.

Breathe into it and ask yourself... what conversation am I having in mind about this decision? What am I afraid of? What is blocking me from moving forward?

_____

_____

_____

_____

_____

_____

_____

_____

_____

_____

_____

_____

Imagine for a moment that the universe is answering your call for help around making this decision. Drop down into your body and really listen. Notice sensations in your body, images or colors you may see with your third eye chakra (your center of intuition), and emotions that come up for you. No judgment, just observation.

Close your eyes and ask yourself: Now that I have the inner guidance required to make this decision, what will my decision be?

_____

_____

_____

_____

_____

_____

_____

_____

_____

_____

_____

Asking for Support

There is a stigma in our society about needing and asking for support. We all have the impression that when we ask for help, it somehow reflects weakness or insecurity, and those are not characteristics that we want to reveal to others. The reality is that we're not supposed to go through this life experience alone. If you want to go after something, you need to acknowledge that you may need support. Most of us reject this idea of asking for help. But when you help someone, it feels good. Everyone raises their mood and vibration when they are either giving or receiving support and kindness.

•∘•⟨⟩•∘•

Reflections

When you don't know how to do something on your own, how do you feel about yourself? Do you beat yourself up? Or do you just stuff the idea away, for a few more years pretending you don't have it?

_____

_____

_____

_____

_____

_____

_____

_____

_____

_____

_____

_____

_____

What's been your story about receiving support in the past?

_____

_____

_____

_____

_____

_____

_____

_____

_____

_____

_____

_____

_____

_____

Now practice creating a new story...what new words can you say to yourself that change your perspective on asking for help? For instance, "the more support I receive from others, the more power I have to create my own destiny."

_____

_____

_____

_____

_____

_____

_____

_____

_____

_____

_____

_____

_____

_____

What areas in your life could use more support from others? Who do you need on your team, or in your tribe, to feel fully supported?

_____

_____

_____

_____

_____

_____

_____

_____

_____

_____

_____

_____

_____

_____

_____

Reclaim Your Goddess Power

You are a consciously awake woman ready to reclaim your Goddess power! Take a moment to think about your life right now. What are your deepest heartfelt desires? What yearnings do you have? What might be possible for your life? Imagine one year from today... what is possible, now that you are learning to tap into your divine feminine power?

Unbound and untangle yourself! It's time to reclaim your power and create the life you desire. You've named your limiting beliefs, released them, and replaced them with positive affirmations. You've reawakened your divine feminine power within and learned how to balance your masculine and feminine energies. This next exercise is going to be about going deep within to connect with your higher self and explore your dreams and desires! Your desires lead to your destiny and your true north—your purpose for being here. It's time to reconnect!

Rediscover what turns you on. Connect with your inner child. Your higher self knows what lights you up. Listen. This is where your feminine power lies. Let it speak to you and listen to its messages.

I know this can feel scary. Allow yourself to feel vulnerable. Breathe and go inward. You have all of the answers inside of you. A feeling of freedom and lightness is your clue that you are on the right path and your thoughts may be leading you astray. Find a thought that feels better than the negative, fearful thought and stick with that. Learn to trust your body, your heart, and your soul. Are you ready to dive in?

Reflections

Who are you at your very core? What is your life truly about?

_____

_____

_____

_____

_____

_____

_____

_____

_____

_____

_____

_____

_____

_____

What are your deepest dreams and desires? What is rising up in you? What courageous creations are you being called to birth right now?

_____

_____

_____

_____

_____

_____

_____

_____

_____

_____

_____

_____

_____

_____

_____

What resources do you need to birth what is rising in you?

How will you go forward with all this goddess energy and make a difference?

_____

_____

_____

_____

_____

_____

_____

_____

_____

_____

_____

_____

_____

GLOW LIKE A GODDESS

When you establish Goddess-activating practices for yourself, like the ones I've included here, you will become more connected to the deeper truth of who you are and start living in alignment with your soul's calling. You will start to get into the flow and GLOW like a Goddess.

You discover confidence in your ability to attract and generate the resources you need to thrive. Your relationships improve. You feel spiritually in tune to your own inner compass. You empower yourself to show up, flourish, and thrive.

There are many ways to practice and flex your Sacred Feminine muscles. I've compiled some of my favorite go-to tools I use when working with my clients. Explore and discover what approaches best support you on your journey.

Simple Mindfulness Practices

Feel Your Emotions. As women, we have learned to bury emotions, because feeling them and expressing them are seen as weak. Time to let that sh*t go, girl, because it's not healthy to stuff all those feelings down inside of you. It is essential that you start to feel and express your emotions without fear of judgment. Let it all hang out!

Lift Others Up. We need to connect and collaborate more with other women. Stop fearing, competing, and comparing ourselves to one another. The universe is abundant, and there is enough for everyone. See the beauty in one another and celebrate one another's accomplishments. We all rise together.

Lead with Your Heart. Most women have suffered pain and trauma and, in doing so, we tend to build walls around our hearts to protect ourselves. I know it is scary to let your guard down and be vulnerable. I'm here to encourage you to let those walls crumble. Open your heart, crack it wide open, and be ready to give and receive freely and without fear. Trust your inner goddess nature, and let love lead the way.

Connect with Mother Nature. Nothing is more grounding than stepping outside to connect with this magnificent Earth gifted to us by Mother Nature. Get off your laptop. Go walk barefoot in the grass, hug a tree, gaze at the moon, and reclaim your sense of balance when you connect to her in this way.

Surround Yourself with Beauty. Goddess energy loves beautiful things. Clean out the clutter and create a sacred space that inspires creativity, an important part of divine femininity. Surround yourself with things that make you happy when you look at them, hear them, or touch or smell them. Activate your sacral chakra, the center for sexual energy.

Nurture Your Body. Remember, you are a divine goddess and a true work of art. Your body is your temple and the only permanent home you will ever have. Nourish it with healthy, nutritious foods and plenty of water. Move it with exercise and show it some divine love. And celebrate all the wonderful sensual and sexual parts of yourself.

Listen to Your Intuition. Tap into your third eye, your intuition, and connection to source. It's how Goddesses learn to communicate with Spirit. Trust the inner voice inside your head and know that all the answers are within you. You just need to listen.

Create Sacred Space. Carve out and commit to quiet time every day to go internal and connect with your higher self. Create a private, sacred space that is just for you and adorn it with angel cards, crystals, candles, and sage. Then lean into the love and meditate, journal, and manifest—and repeat!

Meditate. Countless studies have shown that mindfulness and meditation can positively impact emotional, mental, and physical health. Whether you're looking to reduce stress, improve sleep, strengthen relationships, or just be more focused, a daily meditation practice can help. I have written and recorded my own Just Breathe Meditation Library, including topics ranging from grounding, balancing, chakra clearing, attracting abundance, and practicing self-love and compassion.

Shakti Dance. How long has it been since you danced? Within every woman is the primal source of her power, her inner wild. This Goddess energy propels us into creativity, pleasure, bliss, and rich life experience. She's meant to be emitted, shaken loose, breathed out, lifted up, and unleashed into the universe. Activating your own inner Shakti is the most powerful way to release your wild, feminine spirit and achieve your deepest desires and goals.

Through movement and dance, you can draw upon Shakti to express yourself and catalyze change in your life more freely. With that bold, unapologetic Shakti expression comes a direct window into the true self. And achieving authenticity is precisely why we practice. If you want to awaken your inner goddess, dancing is one of the very best movement techniques you can use. Any form of movement will work. Feminine energy is often described as being like the wind or the ocean, as it's constantly in motion and forever changing.

Move and dance in whatever way feels most natural to you. This exercise is all about getting in tune with your body and allowing it to express itself without fear or inhibition. No judgment. YOU ARE A GODDESS!! Be in the flow of your wild womanhood. Put on the music that moves you and let it go.

Create space and time to reflect on how you can honor your human body more lovingly and kindly.

Connect with Your Chakras

The chakra system originated in India several thousand years ago and was brought to the West through the practice of yoga. Chakra means "wheel" in Sanskrit and refers to energy points in your body. They are thought to be spinning disks of energy that should stay "open" and aligned, as they correspond to bundles of nerves, major organs, and areas of our energetic body that affect our emotional and physical well-being.

There are seven main chakras that run along your spine. Each of these seven main chakras has a corresponding number, name, color, specific area of the spine from the sacrum to the crown of the head, and health focus.

Imagine our body as having a circuit network. The circuit network is made up of arteries, veins, nerves, and the organs they are connected to. According to yogis of ancient times, besides the physical body, there exists a subtle—or energy—body which you can't see or touch, but where all life force energy (or pranayama) flows. The circuit network in the subtle body is made up of chakras through which life force energy flows.

When energy or consciousness flows through these centers either in upward or downward directions, there are different emotions, feelings, and sensations that one experiences. This healthy flow of energy keeps on happening very naturally and spontaneously in life all the time. But when we practice yoga and meditation in its authentic form and maintain a healthy diet and lifestyle, we can maintain the upward rise of energy. When you take the time to consciously connect with these different energetic points, it raises your vibration and mind/body connection and allows you to connect with and harness your inner Sacred Feminine more deeply.

Crystal Magic

Feminine energy is the energy of being, of self-love, compassion, intuition, and flow. Use the crystals listed below to tap into the feminine energy that resides within you. There are so many ways to use crystals, and I recommend experimenting with all of them to see what feels most powerful to you. Some examples are to meditate with them, create a crystal grid to amplify the energy, charge them in water under the full moon, incorporate them into your yoga practice, put them in your bath, place them around your home in different spaces, and wear them in jewelry to carry their energy throughout the day.

Labradorite is one of my favorite crystals because it connects to our intuition and self-discovery. It also raises consciousness and brings universal harmony, creating a shift within you that emanates out into the world.

Rose Quartz is a healing stone associated with the heart chakra and compassionate, peaceful feminine energy. It aids in the re-awakening of your heart to love, reminding you of your capacity to both give and receive unconditional love from yourself, others, and the Universe in general.

Selenite is known to help access your inner goddess and communicate more clearly with your highest self. It's named after the Greek word "selene," which means moon. Selenite will remove energy blockages in your body and help you connect with your Shakti energy.

Moonstone is the divine feminine crystal known for tapping into lunar energy. This crystal helps you connect with your intuition and creates a space of sacred peace, flow, and harmony.

Amazonite is known for merging and balancing both the feminine and masculine energies within you. It helps you harness the power of a warrior while keeping you firmly grounded in femininity, intuition, and love.

Connect to Moon Energy

Moon energy is all about the Sacred Feminine, as it promotes reflection, nurturing, and connection. I host new and full moon sacred ceremonies on a regular basis due to the potency of the energy at those times, and I recommend you find a circle of women to share it with.

You can connect to the moon at any point during its cycle and on your own. My recommendations for connecting to moon energy are as follows:

- Stand in the light of the moon, firmly grounded.
- Hold your hands open above your head.

- Breathe deeply. Ask for the divine light of the moon to embrace you.

- Breathe in the light and the power of the moon and allow it to fill you.

- Allow the moon to illuminate anything you need to see in the moment.

- Release and let go of anything that no longer serves you.

- Set your intentions for what you wish to attract in the month ahead.

- Bring your hands to your heart in gratitude.

Commune with Your Tribe

When women circle up in support of one another, magic happens. Find your sacred feminine community and hold on tight. Those soul sisters will always have your back and be ready to lift you back into the light when you need them most.

Yin/Restorative Yoga

Yin (feminine) energy is restful. It's not about action. It's being open-both open-hearted and open to receiving the gifts of the Universe. Practice quiet activities that inspire reflection, and meditation. Practicing Yin/Restorative Yoga will nurture the sacred feminine.

Goddess Card Readings

One of my favorite ways to start, pause and reflect, and/or end each day is to pull cards for a self-reading. I have so many decks I love, but my main go-to deck is The Sacred Rebels deck, which also has a phone app. Simply close your eyes and breathe while you ask yourself what you need to learn today and then pick 1, 2 or 3 cards to find your answers.

Essential Oil Bath

The element of water is feminine. Soaking in a hot bath connects you with the flow of feminine energy. It encourages you to rest and "just be." Incorporate feminine charging essential oils such as:

- Jasmine: a seductive fragrance that balances feminine energy.
- Ylang Ylang: restores self-love & self-confidence.
- Patchouli: a calming, sedating & relaxing oil.
- Rose: oil of the heart chakra that vibrates on the highest frequency.

It is my sincere hope that you enjoy the Sacred Feminine Practices I've shared and that you find abundant blessings, flow, and deep inner soul connection on your journey of re-awakening your divine feminine shakti energy. Remember to shine bright and let your inner light shine for all to see!

SACRED FEMININE ARCHETYPES

An Archetype forms the basis of all unlearned, instinctive patterns of behavior. These powerful universal symbols exist in what pioneering psychologist Carl Jung referred to as the "collective unconscious." The Archetype we have influences our actions and reactions and explains the major personality differences between women.

Feminine Archetypes are universal patterns of energy found in all of us. Each of us has a primary, and sometimes secondary, Rising Feminine Archetype that corresponds with one of our chakras.

These archetypes represent the potentials that lie within all of us and that we have access to at any time. These archetypes show us the qualities of humanity and how they live within all of us. They are symbols of our higher selves and our human potential.

The High Priestess (Crown Chakra)

The High Priestess is wed to the Divine and serves as a bridge between two worlds, channeling information and creating beauty and harmony through her life's work. High Priestesses are leaders of light in the world. She is so devoted to her purpose that she may find it difficult to put her personal life or relationships first, because she feels such devotion to her calling. High Priestesses in times past were responsible for offering rituals so the sun could rise and set. She feels great responsibility to beauty, balance, and harmony in the world. To serve in a sustainable way, the High Priestess needs to learn to serve herself, which does not come naturally to her.

The Seer (Third Eye Chakra)

The Seer has an astute intuition and an ability to see things others cannot. Like the High Priestess, she is a mystical bridge between the seen world and the unseen world. Highly sensitive, psychic, and visionary, with much intensity, she journeys deep, to dark places, and is not afraid to face the shadows. Her clear vision allows her to cut through any sort of inauthenticity displayed by others. The Seer tends to say it like it is, and her truth speaking can trigger others especially those who are accustomed to living in a world where things are seen but not spoken about.

The Storyteller (Throat Chakra)

The Storyteller is here on this earth to share her stories and opinions with the world freely and without fear of repercussion. She makes an eloquent speaker, writer, performer, and teacher. The passing down of information is what she came here to do. She receives so many ideas from Spirit that she must find a channel through which her creations can be shared. The Storyteller is at her most powerful when she is sharing her wisdom and insights with willing students eager to learn and evolve.

The Healer (Heart Chakra)

The Healer feels things very deeply. She is unconditional with her loving, a natural empath who is highly sensitive to her environment. She has a huge heart and a tender capacity to relate and hold others during their darkest hours. She sees the wholeness of all people and is not quick to judge; you can say just about anything to a Healer and be accepted with love. She can see the good and light in all. The Healer needs to remember that in order to heal others, she must first tend to her own healing, and be open to receiving abundance for her work.

The Warrior (Solar Plexus)

The Warrior is fierce and resilient. She is the game changer and the activist of the world. She possesses remarkable courage and is not afraid to stand up and journey where others are afraid to go. The Warrior is here to bring justice. She cannot be restrained, because she is boundless. The Warrior needs to remember to fight for what she believes in most, rather than to resist what she is against.

The Medicine Woman (Sacral Chakra)

The Medicine Woman has the capacity to journey into the shadows in search of the light. Throughout history, she has been misunderstood as a "witch" and sometimes mistreated. At her essence, she is one with Mother Earth, connected with the cyclic nature of life, and in tune with the seasons, animals, the Moon, and the body. She values the sacredness of all life and knows how to use the five elements to create magic for herself and others.

The Earth Mother (Root Chakra)

The Earth Mother is the midwife of the world. She is here to usher in the new through encouraging, supporting, and assisting others. She is very grounded and ready to birth the expansive potential of the world. She possesses a mother bear-like energy when she needs to protect what is being born. Highly compassionate and attentive, she makes a wonderful friend, always caring for others, and thrives being in a relationship and surrounded by people.

Which one of these Sacred Feminine Archetypes do you most resonate with and why?

_____

_____

_____

_____

_____

_____

_____

_____

_____

_____

_____

_____

MY FAVORITE GODDESSES

The study of the Goddess and the integration of her wisdom is a spiritual path of faith and love. In this connection, we find a reflection of our own soul. Some of my favorite Goddesses are:

Aphrodite (Greek)—Goddess of love and beauty. Daughter of the Sea. No man could resist her. She rules marriages and the love within them.

Artemis (Greek)—Goddess of the hunt, ruler of nature. Also Goddess of childbirth, with the strength and ability to protect herself from unwanted attention.

Asteria (Greek)—Goddess of the Stars, who escaped the advances of Zeus by turning herself into a quail.

Atalanta (Greek)—Competitive Warrior Goddess, adventurous and amazing runner who could not be beaten by a man.

Athena (Greek)—Goddess of war and wisdom. Her name means "mind of God," and she is known for her great intellectual ability to see the true nature of a situation and to develop successful strategies.

Demeter (Greek)—Goddess of the harvest, who possessed great knowledge of the best way to grow, preserve, and harvest grain. Her name means "earth mother."

Devi (Hindu)—Shakti, Goddess of Female Divinity. Mother of the Universe and balance of light and dark.

Diana (Greek)—Goddess of the hunt and wild animals. Her name means "heavenly divine," and she is the guardian of all that is wild and free.

Durga (Hindu)—Radiant Warrior Goddess, the protector of all that is good and harmonious in the world. Sitting astride a lion or tiger, the multi-limbed Durga battles the forces of evil in the world.

Frigg/Freya (Nordic)—Goddess of motherhood and the most beautiful of goddesses. No mortal or God can resist her.

Gaia (Greek)—Goddess of the Earth and all that is fertile.

Hestia (Greek)—Goddess who rules hearth and home, her name means "she dwells."

Hathor (Egyptian)—One of the most ancient goddesses who personifies love, joy, music, dance, motherhood, and fertility.

Ishtar/Inanna (Sumerian)—Goddess of sexual love who ruled over love, fertility, and war. Her name means "goddess of the sky."

Isis (Egyptian)—Goddess of life and magic, the queen of the sky, earth, and moon.

Kali (Hindu)—Fearsome demon-destroying Goddess of time. She is often misunderstood in mythology and cannot be fit into the western narrative of good vs. evil, as she in fact transcends both.

Kuan Yin (Hindu)—Buddhist goddess of mercy, compassion, and healing.

Lakshmi (Hindu)—Goddess of abundance, prosperity, and spiritual wealth.

Luna (Roman) – Goddess of the moon.

Persephone (Greek) – Goddess of the underworld, the abode of death.

Rhea (Greek) – Ancient Titan earth goddess responsible for the fertility of the soil and women.

Saraswati (Hindu) – Goddess of knowledge, language, and the arts.

Venus (Roman) – Goddess of love and beauty.

Who is your favorite Goddess and why? What characteristics does she represent that resonate with you?

ACKNOWLEDGEMENTS

I would like to thank Source for downloading the wisdom and giving me the push beyond my comfort zone to put my story out there to help others heal.

I am proud of my wounded inner child for learning to love herself after years of hiding behind shame and grief.

I would like to thank my biological and adopted parents, and family, for providing me with opportunity, as well as obstacles, from which to learn, grow, and evolve.

Deep gratitude to my Soul Sisters for always having my back, and to Jo for inspiring me from Spirit to go big or go home.

Love and appreciation to David, for not giving up on me as I worked through my own unresolved trauma and feelings of unworthiness.

To my daughter and divine inspiration, Nataliya: you are the light of my life. May you continue to see the world in all its brilliance, from the heart of the Artist, and allow yourself the freedom to paint your landscape using all the colors!

ABOUT THE AUTHOR

Jennifer Gulbrand is an author, speaker, podcast host, and builder of communities and safe, supportive containers. She founded the SheBreathes Balance Women's Collaborative and the WeBreathe Wellness Retreat Center in Massachusetts, to hold space for growth and healing, to raise the collective vibration, and to help heal the human heart. In her private practice as a trauma-informed somatic therapy practitioner and empowerment coach, she guides women back into better alignment with their true nature.

She combines her work as a Spiritual Guide and Energy and Vibrational Sound Healer to improve the lives of her clients by helping them find more complete balance in body, mind and spirit. She is the creator and host of the High Vibes + Grateful Heart podcast for women on the rise. When she's not writing, creating content, or teaching, you will find her at the beach, traveling, or in sacred ceremonies with her tribe of soul sisters.